W9-BUF-867

KIN   TEN

by Cheryl Gorder

Irvin L. Young Memorial Library
Whitewater, Wisconsin

Kindergarten at Home

Published by:

Blue Bird Publishing

2266 S. Dobson #275
Mesa AZ 85202
(602) 831-6063 FAX (602) 831-1829
Email: bluebird@bluebird1.com
Web Site: www.bluebird1.com

ISBN 0-933025-53-X
$22.95

Library of Congress Cataloging-in-Publication Data

Gorder, Cheryl, 1952-
    Kindergarten at home / by Cheryl Gorder.
        p. cm.
    Includes bibliographical references (p.).
    ISBN 0-933025-53-X
    1. Home schooling--United States. 2. Kindergarten--United States-
Curricula. 3. Kindergarten--Activity programs--United States.
I. Title.
LC40.G689 1997
371-04'2--dc21
                                       97-11494
                                         CIP

About the Author

Cheryl Gorder has been involved with home schooling since 1983, when she began homeschooling her daughter, Sarah. In 1985, Cheryl wrote the book *Home Schools: An Alternative* which has become a homeschooling classic and a bestseller. The book is in its fourth edition. She wrote that book because information about home education was hard to find, and she wanted information available to people who were interested.

Cheryl began homeschooling her daughter because of extensive traveling, but soon found that there were other compelling reasons to home school. These ideas became the foundation of the home schooling books she has written, which include *Home Education Resource Guide*, now in its fourth edition.

Sarah thrived with home education. At fifteen, she began college. She has been an "A" student at Arizona State University, and has participated in many extraordinary experiences. She had an internship at the Smithsonian Institution in Washington, D.C., working with world-renown experts in her field of archaeology. She has studied in Kenya, Africa at the famous Koobi Fora field school conducted by Harvard. She is involved with the Americorps program in Mesa, Arizona, and has been developing educational programs for children. Cheryl works with Sarah as a volunteer in the after-school enrichment programs in Mesa.

Cheryl has continued writing, editing, and publishing books. Her other books include: *Green Earth Resource Guide, Multicultural Education Resource Guide, Home Business Resource Guide* and *Homeless: Without Addresses in America,* which won a prestigious Benjamin Franklin award in 1989.

Cheryl is often a guest on radio and TV shows discussing homeschooling, and is available to speak at conventions and seminars.

Dedication

To my daughter, Sarah,
who has been the greatest joy of my life
and an inspiration for my writing
and to my mother, Arlene,
for showing me how a mother should be.

Table of Contents

Index of Activities Listed by Page Number

Materials Needed to Teach This Program

The materials needed for this program are generally commonly available household objects. Provide a box to keep the materials and supplies, such as crayons, glue, scissors, pencil, and paper. Teach your child to put things away when finished. This teaches organizational skills and responsibility.

Crayons
Paint
Paint Brush
White Glue
Construction Paper
Paper Plates
Modeling Clay
Tape Recorder (Optional)
Markers or Colored Pencils
Building Blocks

Muffin Pan
Wooden Blocks
Butcher Paper
Buttons
Jars
Blunt Scissors
Scraps of Fabric
Fishing Line
Magnet
Straws

Sandpaper
White Paper
Newspaper
Old Shirt
Sand
Masking Tape
Pencils
Easel (Optional)
Bulletin Board

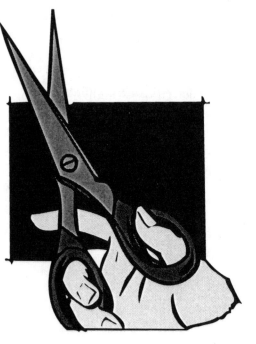

Introduction for the Parent/Teacher

The parent is the child's most important teacher.

Each child is unique and learns in different ways and at different rates, just as all children grow at different rates physically. Because they know more about their child than anyone else, parents are the first and best teachers a child has.

The activities in this book will help you do an even better job of developing your child's intellect and learning readiness. With your help and this book, your child can acquire many of the basic learning skills essential for future success in school.

Children learn by being actively involved.

Children learn through being actively involved in a variety of experiences. Young children have a surprising capacity for learning and are eager learners. Give them that opportunity.

Children learn at different rates.

Since your child is unique, he or she will not develop the same skills at the same time as any other child. Do not compare your child to anyone else. Developing a basic learning skill may take time, especially if your child is not ready for a specific activity. Don't worry about it; go on to the next activity. Always use appropriate praise to encourage your child.

Follow the easy directions.

The directions for these activities are simple and easy to follow, with clear illustrations. Feel free to extend activities if your child is interested. Do not overstimulate or overtire your child. Come back to the activities another day, if necessary. You should plan on doing three activities daily, working with your child about an hour each day. Make sure you schedule your activities on a regular basis.

Why Kindergarten at Home?

There are many reasons to kindergarten at home:

(1) Your child is still bonding with you. Allowing this bond to strengthen helps the child develop his self-identity which in turn keeps him away from negative peer pressure in later years.

(2) Your child is developing at his own individual rate. By keeping him at home for kindergarten, you allow his development to proceed naturally, without forcing him into a mold.

(3) Your child will not be influenced by the bad behaviors, bad attitudes, and violence found in the public schools.

(4) The home is the most natural and loving environment for learning.

(5) The homeschooled children of today will be the leaders of tomorrow!

The advantages of this kindergarten-at-home book lie in its interactive lessons. This is not a workbook with repetitive drills, but rather an active learning guide for parent and child. These kinds of learning activities are designed to help your child become a well-rounded individual.

For more information about homeschooling, please check our Web Site at: www.bluebird1.com

How to Tell if Your Child
is Ready for Kindergarten

Many parents wonder if their child is going to be ready for kindergarten. You want your child to be successful and to be able to learn to read with ease and enthusiasm.

Learning to read does start in the home and continues during the child's school years. Just as your child naturally learns to talk by following your example, your child may naturally learn a great deal about reading long before ever setting foot in the classroom.

How can parents be assured that their child has the necessary skills and general knowledge for learning to read and being a successful student? Answer these questions honestly, and you can decide for yourself if your child is ready for kindergarten. Read each question carefully, and if you can say yes to these 20 questions, then you'll have no problem.

1. Following directions: My child is able to listen and follow three-step directions. Example: "Put this pencil on the table, open the door, and come back and sit by me."
2. Good expressive oral language: My child has good expressive oral language. My child is able to speak in complete sentences and be understood.
3. Body parts: My child is able to name these body parts: eyes, nose, ears, stomach, foot, head, knee, finger, shoulder, and mouth.
4. Able to count: My child is able to count 1-10 and is able to name each number, 1-10, in isolation.
5. Geometric figures: My child is able to name and draw the square, circle, triangle, and straight line.
6. Identify basic colors: My child is able to identify and name the basic colors, red, brown, yellow, orange, purple, black, and white.
7. Important words: My child is able to use these important words: first, last, front, middle, smaller, lighter, and between.
8. Self-identification: My child knows first name, last name, telephone number, and address and can tell where he/she lives.
9. General knowledge: My child has good general knowledge, such as where we buy food, what a doctor does, what a teacher does, where we get gas, and what a school is.
10. Body coordination: My child does not fall frequently. My child can walk a straight line, stand on one foot, and skip.
11. Hold a pencil: My child is able to hold a pencil or crayon correctly.
12. Knows alphabet: My child is able to name and identify the letters of the alphabet.
13. Social skills: My child has good social skills. My child is accepted by other children, is able to anticipate the outcome of inappropriate behavior, know right from wrong, assumes

responsibility for behavior, knows how to play fair, is able to follow rules when playing games, and has good personal hygiene.

14. Good health: My child has good general health, a good appetite, and adequate energy. My child gets good exercise and eight to nine hours of sleep each night.
15. Is happy: My child is happy most of the time and feels secure.
16. Manners: My child uses and knows what good manners are.
17. Listening skills: My child can listen to a story for 10 or 15 minutes without getting restless.
18. Follows rules: My child can follow rules and do what he/she is told to do.
19. Balance board: My child is able to walk on a curb or a straight line.
20. Classifying: My child is able to group items, such as fruit and vegetables or colored clothes and white clothes, according to color and function.

Give your child five points for each of the above items, and you will have an indication of how your child will do when starting kindergarten.

Scoring:
100-90: Will be very successful, will enjoy school and learning should be easy.
90-80: Your child will be a good learner and probably be an above average student.
80-70: Will do about average work at school and may have trouble keeping up with some of the class members.
70-60: Will have to struggle and be working at his/her frustration level and will probably become a behavior problem and will not be a successful student.
60 and below: Your child will have serious problems and not be a successful learner. Have your child evaluated by a professional and follow their advice.

When children experience failure, it is very, very hard for them to overcome failure. They frequently feel dumb and stupid and may give up. Your child's first experience with learning must be good and happy, or poor behavior and acting out will be the results.

Frequently, the teacher and school is blamed for a child's failure. If you feel your child is not ready for school, you should have an honest conference with the principal. You may want to consider keeping your child home another year. Your child may be a late bloomer and need some more time to grow and develop.

General Principals for Teaching Kindergarten

1. Do the activities with the child and enjoy them.
2. Learn to give appropriate praise and to be positive.
3. Avoid anger and criticism.
4. Make sure these activities are enjoyable, nonthreatening, and nonstressful.
5. Keep this book close at hand and do the activities at the same time each day.
6. Always read through directions and have materials ready before each activity.
7. Be sure you have scheduled your time so you can finish the activity. Do the activity at the same time every day, so it becomes routine.
8. Avoid pressure. Do not force a child to do any activity. If the child is not ready for an activity, do it some other day.
9. Fantasy and imagination are to be encouraged as long as the child recognizes the differences between fantasy and reality.
10. When doing art activities, spread newspaper over and under the work space.
11. Always clean up afterwards together, washing brushes and cups and storing materials appropriately, while discussing the activity. This teaches your child responsibility.
12. Teach the child songs and poems and have the child teach them to other members of the family to build traditions.
13. Supervise activities, and especially if there is any danger.
14. Dress your child appropriately for the activity.
15. Check outdoor areas for sharp or hazardous materials.
16. Continually educate your child about being safe.
17. Always let children come up with their own ideas and creativity.
18. Discover with your child the wonders of the world; encourage discussion about feelings. Avoid remarks that hinder communication, such as, "Yes, I know that," or "I don't have time now."
19. Sharpen your listening skills and practice listening to your child; talk daily to each other; always listen.
20. Be a good role model for your child.

Reading To Your Child

You should read to your child every day for at least 15 minutes. Read a variety of books: poetry, fairytales, humorous, fanciful, high adventure, and factual stories.

The activities section will occasionally have a reading activity to remind you to read to your child. However, the best policy is not to wait for these activities, but rather to make it a practice to set aside at least 15 minutes regularly everyday to read to your child.

The **bibliography** has lists of recommended reading books in many categories.

Tips for Reading to Your Child:
(1) Show interest as you read. Make reading a pleasureable experience.
(2) Find a time when you and your child are relaxed and interested in reading; bedtime or after a nap is ideal.
(3) Let your child choose the book or pages to read.
(4) Point to the pictures as you talk about them.
(4) Let your child hold the book and turn the pages as you read.
(5) Tell a familiar story, but leave out words or parts of sentences for your child to fill in.
(6) Write down your child's homemade story and read it aloud.
(7) Let your child make up a story or finish one you have started.
(8) If your child does not show interest in listening to a story, continue to read as your child plays quietly. Eventually, your child will again be interested in participating and listening.

Wordless Books:
(1) These are books that have no text, but each picture tells the next step in the story. A list of wordless books is in the bibiography.
(2) These are excellent for having the child make up the story as he views the pictures. You can also write down the story he tells, and read it to him later.

READ TO YOUR CHILD EVERY DAY!

ACTIVITIES

-1-

NAME WALL HANGING

Purpose: To develop name and alphabet recognition.
Materials Needed: Poster board or cardboard, drinking
glass, crayons or markers, ribbon or yarn.

Parent/ Teacher: This activity will help your child take pride in his name.

Directions:

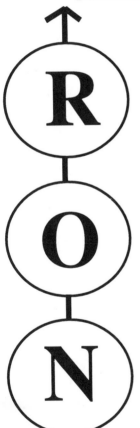

(1) Using a drinking glass, draw circles on poster board or cardboard. Make as many circles as there are letters in your child's name.
(2) Cut out the circles.
(3) Using crayons markers, have the child write a letter on each circle. Have him spell out his name.
(4) Decorate the circles.
(5) Attach yarn or ribbon between each circle and at the top so that the name can hang.
(6) If you wish, attach a long sheet of paper or posterboard behind the circle and decorate it too.

-2-

SORTING GROCERIES

> **Purpose: To learn how to sort and classify.**
> **Materials Needed: Bag of groceries.**

Parent/ Teacher: A trip to the grocery store provides a fun learning experience that teaches an important skill—classifying.

Directions:

(1) Have the child sort the groceries by classifications such as vegetables, fruits, dairy products, cereals, and canned goods.
(2) Help the child classify the products and put them in sorted piles.
(3) Do not criticize the child if she does not classify them the same way you would, but gently correct her.
(4) Ask your child if there could be a different way to classify the groceries, and then you sort them according to her classification.
(5) Praise your child when she does well.

-3-

MAGNET SCIENCE

Purpose: To learn basic science skills.
Materials Needed: Magnet, paper clips, nails,
buttons, pins, glass objects, small toys, and
various objects.

Parent/ Teacher: Try this activity with many kinds of objects.

Directions:

(1) Explain to your child what a magnet is—
that it attracts only things made of iron and steel.
(2) Use the magnet to lift a nail.
(3) Try lifting a glass object, and explain to the
child why the magnet will not lift it.
(4) Have the child try to lift different objects.
(5) What else can your child find that a magnet
will stick to?

-4-

FISHING FOR LETTERS

> **Purpose: To develop alphabet recognition.**
> **Materials Needed: Stick, construction paper,**
> **   string, magnet, paper clips, and a box.**

Parent/ Teacher: Variations of this game include using it for numbers, easy addition problems, and shapes.

Directions:

(1) Make a fishing pole using a stick, string, and a magnet on the end.

(2) Cut out fish of many shapes from colored construction paper. Write a letter on each one.

(3) Put a paper clip on each fish.

(4) Put all the fish in a box and call it your fish pond.

(5) Catch a fish with your pole. What letter is it?

(6) Have your child fish for letters. To make a game for early readers, you can catch enough fish to make a word. First person to make a real word with the letters they catch gets a cooky!

-5-

PAPER PLATE CLOCK

Purpose: To learn how to tell time.
Materials Needed: Paper plate, cardboard, scissors,
**   pencil, crayons or markers, fastener.**

Parent/ Teacher: Several clocks can be made for different times
of the day, such as breakfast, lunch, dinner, and bedtime. They can
be put on the refrigerator to look at again and again. Refrigerators were
made to put children's art on!

Directions:

(1) On the paper plate, draw the numbers of the clock.
It helps to show the child that a circle can be divided into
halves and quarters by placing first the 12, then the 6, then
the 3 and then the 9. Fill in the rest of the numbers.
(2) Make arrows out of cardboard for the hour hand and
the minute hand.
(3) Fasten the arrows on the plate.
(4) Talk about time and what happens at what time of day.
(6) Make a game by putting on index cards the following
questions, one per card, and then take turns showing the
answers on the clock.

a. What time does Dad get home from work?
b. What time is breakfast?
c. What time is dinner?
d. What time is bedtime?

-6-

MY FAMILY

> **Purpose: To develop self-recognition.**
> **Materials Needed: Construction paper, crayons or markers, scissors.**

Parent/ Teacher: The first part of social skills is having the child recognize who he is, who his family is, and how he fits in. You should also explain that families may be different from each other, may change size, and how families change.

Directions:

(1) With the construction paper, cut out a house or some other figure that your child recognizes and associates with home.

(2) Write several sentences on the house showing who the child is. Ask the child the following questions and then write the answers on the house.

      a. Who am I?

      b. What is my dad's name?

      c. What is my mom's name?

      d. What are the names of my brothers and sisters?

      e. Where do I live?

(3) Discuss relationships such as grandmother, grandfather, aunt, uncle, nephew, and niece.

(4) Role play the parts of the family, each one taking a turn being grandmother, baby sister, daddy, etc.

-7-

FOOD TRAIN

> **Purpose:** To learn how to tell food groups and nutrition, vocabulary.
>
> **Materials Needed:** 5 boxes (milk cartons or shoe boxes work well), construction paper, scissors, stapler, straws, string, magazines, markers.

Parent/ Teacher: This is a good activity to do with more than one child.

Directions:

(1) Cut the top or side off the boxes. Keep in mind that each box will be one car of the train.
(2) Tape or glue construction paper on the sides of the box. Make the cars various colors: blue, red, yellow.
(3) Wheels can be made by inserting straws and attaching wheels made of construction paper or cardboard.
(4) Make an engine.
(5) Attach the engine and the cars together with string.
(6) Label the cars by food groups: "meat," "bread," "dairy products," and "fruits and vegetables."
(7) Have the child cut food pictures from magazines and then put them in the proper train cars.
(8) With several children, this can become a game. When a child correctly puts a food into its proper category, he becomes the "conductor" with the train and gets to ask the next child, the "passenger" which car he's going to. In order to become the "'conductor," the child must be able to put a food into its proper car.

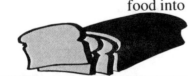

-8-

READING TO YOUR CHILD

Purpose: To develop listening skills, left-to-right eye movement, vocabulary, general knowledge, love of reading, auditory discrimination, visual discrimination, thinking skills, imagination, oral language skills, promotes parent and child bonding, and improves the child's capacity for learning.

Materials Needed: Book to read. Select one from the bibiography or let your child choose.

Parent/ Teacher: Read to your child every day for at least 15 minutes. Many families like to have reading time just before bedtime or at bedtime. Some children enjoy spontaneous reading time. You need to find the time that is best for you and your child.

Tips on Choosing Books:

(1) Stories should be appropriate for the child's age. They will enjoy Mother Goose, nursery stories, and other books describing familiar objects and experiences.

(2) They will enjoy listening to slightly complex texts with good rhythm and effective word repetition. Dr. Seuss books are excellent for this.

(3) The books you and your child select should help add new words to the child's vocabulary. Explain clearly what new words mean and how to properly pronounce them.

(4) Your public librarian can help you select books for reading to your child, or see the bibliography in the back of this book.

-9-

BOOK OF SOUNDS

Purpose: To develop alphabet recognition.
Materials Needed: Magazines, scissor, paper, glue or
tape.

Parent/ Teacher: A similar book can be made for numbers.

Directions:

(1) Staple together 13 sheets of paper. On each page, you will be doing one letter of the alphabet. (Front and back, 13 x 2 is 26 letters).

(2) On each page, write a letter of the alphabet, both captial letter and small letter.

(3) Have your child pick pictures from magazines that represent the sounds of each letter, and paste them in the book.

(4) For a book on numbers, write the number (1) and then the name (one). Do numbers 1-20.

-10-

NUMBER WORM

> **Purpose: To develop number recognition.**
> **Materials Needed: Construction paper, crayons or markers, scissors.**

Parent/ Teacher: The activity can be used for learning other skills as well, such as word recognition. When you child is ready to read simple words, put words on the worm instead of numbers.

Directions:

(1) With the construction paper, cut out a several oval pieces.

(2) Write a number on each one, from 1 to 10. Attach the pieces together to make a worm. Make a funny face and add to the worm.

(3) Place the worm on the bulletin board and frequently ask the child to count the number worm.

(4) When the child has mastered counting to 10, make a new number worm from 11 to 20.

-11-

MY TOWN

Purpose: To develop social awareness.
Materials Needed: None.

Parent/ Teacher: Another part of social skills is having the child recognize where she lives and that she lives in a town or city with a name.

Directions:

(1) Take a drive through your town or city.
(2) Tell your child the name your town. Tell her how the town was named.
(3) As you're driving, show her important landmarks.
(4) Go the Chamber of Commerce and find literature and maps of your town.
(5) Go to the airport and explain that's one way how people come and go to your town or city.

-12-

BUILDING WITH BLOCKS

Purpose: To develop coordination, shape recognition, hand-to-eye coordination.
Materials Needed: Building blocks.

Parent/ Teacher: Sometimes what seems like play is really the best way a child learns. Allow the child to play with educationally-oriented toys. Items like building blocks teach numerous skills.

Directions:

(1) Allow the child to build his own creation with the blocks.

(2) Ask the child questions about what he is doing and why he is doing it. You can build his vocabulary by teaching him shapes, designs, and styles about what he is building.

(3) Ask him to tell you a story about the structure he has created. If it's a house, who lives in it? If it's a castle, is there a princess?

-13-

HAPPY MUSIC

Purpose: To develop interest in music and an understanding of people's moods.
Materials Needed: None.

Parent/ Teacher: Sing this famliar song with zest, following the directions in each verse. When the song calls for being happy, show an exaggerated grin. When it calls for being angry, show an exaggerated face. This not only teaches the child, but is lots of fun!

If You're Happy And You Know It

If you're happy and you know it, clap your hands (clap clap).
If you're happy and you know it, clap your hands (clap clap).
If you're happy and you know it, then your face will surely show it.
If you're happy and you know it, clap your hands (clap clap).

If you're angry and you know it, stomp your feet (stomp stomp).
If you're angry and you know it, stomp your feet (stomp stomp).
If you're angry and you know it, then your face will surely show it.
If you're angry and you know it, stomp your feet (stomp stomp).

If you're weary and you know it, heave a sigh (whee ooo).
If you're weary and you know it, heave a sigh (whee ooo).
If you're weary and you know it, then your face will surely show it.
If you're weary and you know it, heave a sigh (whee ooo).

If you're joyous and you know it, click your heels (click click).
If you're joyous and you know it, click your heels (click click).
If you're joyous and you know it, then your face will surely show it.
If you're joyous and you know it, click your heels (click click).

-14-

SEQUENCE ACTIVITIES

Purpose: To develop a sense of how things are ordered and sequenced.
Materials Needed: Paper towel tubes, blocks.

Parent/ Teacher: Try to show order using many different objects until the child understands the concept.

Directions:

(1) Cut paper towel tubes different lengths. Have the child put them in order from shortest to longest.
(2) Have your child put building blocks in order from shortest to longest or smallest to shortest.
(3) Have your child put your family members in order from smallest to largest.
(4) Ask your child to show "first" and "last" in pages of a magazine.

-15-

SHADOW PUPPETS

Purpose: To develop science and thinking skills.
Materials Needed: Light.

Parent/ Teacher: Encourage children to act out stories with their puppets.

Directions:

(1) Turn off the lights, and shine a bright light onto a wall or a white piece of paper.
(2) Show your children how to make hand shadows on the wall.
(3) Explain how shadows are made—by blocking light.
(4) Ask your child why she can't see her shadow on a cloudy day. Ask your child what time of day her shadow is the longest.

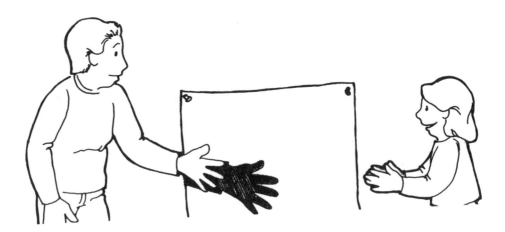

-16-

SHOW ME

> **Purpose: To develop motor skills, oral communication.**
> **Materials Needed: None.**

Parent/ Teacher: This is a good activity to do outdoors, perhaps with a picnic in the park.

Directions:

    (1) Ask the child:

        "Show me how tall you can be."

        "Show me how thin you can be."

        "Show me how fast you can be."

        "Show me how slow you can walk."

    (2) You child can ask you "show me" as well.

    (3) Blindfold your child, and ask:

        "Show me where the tree is."

        "Show me where the car is."

-17-

HIGH AND LOW

Purpose: To develop spatial concepts.
Materials Needed: None.

Parent/ Teacher: Think of animals for the child to demonstrate these concepts. The next activity (ZOO) is a good time to teach these concepts.

Directions:

(1) Direct the child to wave his hands high, then low.
(2) Ask your child to name an animal moves low to the ground (snake) and demonstrate that animal.
(3) Ask him to name an animal is high off the ground (giraffe) and then demonstrate the animal.

-18-

VISITING THE ZOO

> **Purpose: To add general knowledge, to practive creative movement and creative dramatics.**
> **Materials Needed: A zoo trip.**

Parent/ Teacher: After visiting the zoo, you and your child can act like one of the animals. Act out the animal's behavior.

Directions:

(1) Be an angry lion waking up, roaring loudly, and pacing back and forth.
(2) Be an elephant eating hay with his long trunk or taking a dirt bath.
(3) Be a tall giraffe eating leaves and stems off the trees and spreading his front legs to take a drink.
(4) Be a kangaroo with a baby in her pouch, jumping around in a circle.

-19-

FLY LIKE A BIRD

Purpose: To develop muscles, coordination, and oral language.
Materials Needed: None.

Parent/ Teacher: Exercises like these can be as creative as you wish. Even though it seems like play, there are many skills being learned.

Directions:

(1) Ask your child to pretend to fly like a bird. Make your arms wave about and fly with her. Act like you're landing on a branch.
(2) Ask your child to hop like a frog. Hop along with her. This builds many important muscles for your child.
(3) Ask her to stretch like a lion waking up in the morning.
(4) Ask her to swim like a fish, hop like a rabbit, or soar like an eagle.

-20-

THE ME TREE

> **Purpose: To develop a sense of self.**
> **Materials Needed: Construction paper, crayons, scissors, magazines, tape or glue.**

Parent/ Teacher: Encourage the child to find as many things about himself to put on the tree as possible.

Directions:

(1) Cut out a large tree from construction paper.
(2) Have the child decorate the tree to show his personality and interests. It's HIS tree. He can be as creative as he wants.
(3) He can cut pictures from magazines and glue them to the tree or draw items to add.
(4) Put the tree on the bulletin board. Encourage him to add items on later days.

-21-

VISIT A DRY CLEANING STORE

> **Purpose: To develop career awareness and oral vocabulary.**
> **Materials Needed: None.**

Parent/ Teacher: Field trips are very important. Take as many as you can. Teach your child how different people earn their living, and let them talk to people doing their jobs.

Directions:

(1) Arrange in advance to bring your child to the dry cleaning store. Ask them if they will spend a couple of minutes showing a child what they do there.

(2) When you bring your child, have her notice the different smells there are. Point out the different machines that are used.

(3) Have her watch someone used a pressing machine.

(4) Watch the clerks check in and out clothing for cleaning.

-22-

PEOPLE AT WORK

Purpose: To develop career awareness.
Materials Needed: Construction paper, magazines,
  glue, crayons, scissors.

Parent/ Teacher: Career awareness should start very young. Over the years, your child will show interest in several different careers before choosing a path later in life. That is perfectly normal. Allow your child to know as many kinds of work as possible.

Directions:

(1) Make a poster of different kinds of work by cutting magazines picture and glueing them to construction paper.
(2) Write the name of the job under the picture.
(3) Discuss the kinds of work the people do.
(4) Visit people at work.

-23-

MAKE MUSIC WITH MARACAS

Purpose: To develop an interest in musical instruments.
Materials Needed: Small juice can or cardboard tube,
rubber bands, beans or macaroni, construction
paper.

Parent/ Teacher: Try the maracas with different kinds of music.

Directions:

(1) Cover one end of the cardboard tube with construction paper or aluminum foil. Secure with rubber band or tape.
(2) Fill the tube with beans or macaroni.
(3) Cover the other end.
(4) Decorate with construction paper or streams of crepe paper.
(5) Shake the maracas to the beat of the music. Find some music with a good strong beat. Reggae is especially good for this.

-24-

OBSTACLE COURSE

Purpose: To develop muscle control, physical education and following directions.
Materials Needed: None.

Parent/ Teacher: This is especially good for several children, as they can become a train. Try to make this course challenging for the children.

Directions:

(1) Create an obstacle course in your home or in the yard by using old tires, boxes, chairs, ropes, bikes, and other objects.
(2) Lead your child around the obstacle course, first slowly, then more rapidly. Make sure that there are no objects that would injure the child if he fell.
(3) Create a story about what you're doing and where you're going. "We're on a train going to Grandma's house."

-25-

ETHNIC EVENT

> **Purpose: To develop a sense of diversity.**
> **Materials Needed: None.**

Parent/ Teacher: Children need to know that people are different in many ways, and that difference is normal and good. When we teach our children at home, we need to give them many chances to participate in the outside world so that they can observe these differences and come to accept them. A good book for materials for teaching diversity is *Multicultural Education Resource Guide* from Blue Bird Publishing.

Directions:

(1) Take the child to an ethnic event, such as a Greek Festival, an Irish Festival, Cinco de May celebration, Native American Pow-Wow, or a Martin Luther King Day celebration. Make an effort to go to these when they occur in your area.

(2) Show your child on the globe where the ethnic group lives or originated from.

(3) Explain that differences among people are normal and good. Show how there are differences even within your own family.

(4) At the event, sample ethnic food and look at ethnic crafts.

(5) Encourage the child to ask questions of artists and craftspeople at these events.

-26-

WATER RAINBOWS

Purpose: To develop science thinking and oral language.
Materials Needed: Water hose.

Parent/ Teacher: Try to show order using many different objects until the child understands the concept.

Directions:

(1) On a sunny day, use a hose and spray a fine mist in the air. Have your child stand where she can see a rainbow forming.
(2) Have the child stand in different positions to see where the rainbow forms and where it does not.
(3) Ask her what colors she sees in the rainbow.
(4) Explain how the colors are formed.
(5) Your child can later paint a rainbow to make her own rainbow poster.

-27-

MACARONI NAMES

Purpose: To learn to spell his name, to develop visual discrimination.

Materials Needed: Dry macaroni, glue, paper.

Parent/ Teacher: This activity can also be done with other materials, such as spaghetti, herbs, cake decorating bits.

Directions:

(1) Help your child spell his name with macaroni.
(2) Encourage your child to glue the macaroni on paper in the shape of his name.

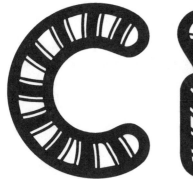

-28-

PERSONAL CHARACTERISTICS

Purpose: To develop self-awareness and create a sense of self-identification.
Materials Needed: Pen and paper.

Parent/ Teacher: Have a discussion about how each person is different. Look at differences between people. Be sure that the child understands that differences are good.

Directions:

(1) Ask your child, "What color hair do you have?"
(2) List the color of your child's hair on a piece of paper.
(3) Continue asking questions about eye color, size, teeth, glasses, etc., and recording the information.
(4) You may also make a list for a friend or a family member.
(5) Discuss the differences in personal characteristics of the people on the list.
(6) Emphasize how differences between people are normal and good.

-29-

FUN WITH SCISSORS

> **Purpose: To develop finger coordination, and to recognize shapes.**
> **Materials Needed: Construction paper, scissors, glue.**

Parent/ Teacher: This activity can be modified to making snowflakes with white paper. In doing that, you use a piece of paper that starts with a circle, and keep folding it in half several times. Cut shapes out of the folded edges. When you unfold it, it looks like a snowflake.

Directions:

(1) Fold a piece of construction paper in half lengthwise.
(2) Holding the paper in one hand, and the scissors in the other, cut shapes out of the folded edge.
(3) When you open up the paper, there will be shapes cutout in the paper. Discuss with your child what kinds of shapes they are.
(4) You can put a different color piece of construction paper behind this one. Additional art can be added with pictures glued on or colored.

-30-

LISTENING

Purpose: To develop listening, sequence, and
   language art skills.
Materials Needed: None.

Parent/ Teacher: These exercises also help the child develop memory skills.

Directions:

(1) Describe a scene, and then have the child draw each item in its proper location.
(2) Example: "The house was beside a barn. Inside the barn was a horse. The sun was high in the sky."
(3) The child should draw these in the proper location.
(4) Make several sounds and have your child repeat the sounds in sequence.
(5) Example: tap your toes, clap your hands, hum. Then ask the child to do it in the same order.
(6) Increase gradually the number of things you do before asking the child to repeat the sequence.

-31-

WHAT IS MONEY?

Purpose: To learn the function of money, to tell how numbers and money are related.
Materials Needed: Coins, paper money, paper, crayons.

Parent/ Teacher: Throughout this activity, explain to your child the concept of money, what it means, how it is used, what it is worth, and how it is related to numbers.

Directions:

(1) Show your child a coin. Ask your child what kind of coin it is. What is it worth? How much can it buy? Look at pennies, nickels, dimes and quarters.
(2) Have the child draw a picture on paper of paper money and color it.
(3) How much is paper money worth? What will it buy?
(4) Show the child bills in other denominations and discuss them.

-32-

HOMES

> **Purpose: To develop oral language and to understand basic human needs.**
> **Materials Needed: Paper, crayons.**

Parent/ Teacher: This activity can also show the kinds of houses used in other countries and by other ethnic groups.

Directions:

(1) Ask your child what a house is for. "Why do you live in a house?" Discuss other kinds of houses: apartments, farm houses, motels, trailers, boats, tipis, igloos, hogans, castles.
(2) Ask the child if animals have houses. What are their houses like? Talk about bird houses, barns, nests, burrows, and other kinds of animal homes.
(3) Ask your child to name as many kinds of houses as possible for both people and animals.
(4) Your child can draw these on paper and color them.
(5) Give your child a chance to discuss her ideas about homes for people and animals. If she want to tell a story, you can write it down for her.

-34-

CLOUD WATCHING

Purpose: To learn science concepts and oral language.
Materials Needed: None except partly cloudy day.

Parent/ Teacher: This activity can be done during a picnic or outing to the park.

Directions:

(1) Lie on the ground with your child and look up at the clouds.

(2) Your child may ask questions about the clouds. Answer the questions clearly but simply.

(3) Ask your child these questions: How do clouds move? What makes clouds? Why are the clouds different colors? What kinds of clouds are there?

(4) Explain the kinds of clouds that bring rain, and which do not bring rain.

(5) Ask the child to make an oral story about clouds.

-34-

PERSONAL GROOMING

**Purpose: To develop good grooming, personal habits and a sense of responsibility.
Materials Needed: Household materials.**

Parent/ Teacher: Have a discussion with your child about the importance of being neat and clean. Personal grooming helps the child develop good self-concept and is best learn by example.

Directions:

(1) Show your child how to take care of his clothes, how to hang them up, how to fold them for the dresser, where to put dirty clothes.
(2) Your child needs to see your taking good care of your clothing. Explain why you do it.
(3) Show your child the washer and dryer and explain that's how clothes are kept clean.

-35-

WHERE I LIVE

> **Purpose:** To learn to spell his name, to develop self-concept and for safety skills.
> **Materials Needed:** Paper and pencil.

Parent/ Teacher: It is important for your child to understand who he is, who his parents are, and his address and phone number. Practice this over and over.

Directions:

(1) Teach your child how to spell his name, address, and phone number.
(2) Explain how important it is for him to know these things.
(3) Explain the if he is lost, he should look for a safe person, such as a police office, teacher, or someone he trusts to give this information to.

My name is Billy Jones.
I live at 443 South 6th Street.
My phone number is 555-0626.

-36-

WRITING THE ALPHABET

Purpose: To develop alphabet skills, writing skills, and language arts.
Materials Needed: Pencil and paper.

Parent/ Teacher: This book is not full of worksheets for repetitive drills on numbers and alphabet. However, these are skills that need repetition. We suggest workbooks such as ESP's *Kindergarten Super Workbook* or workbooks you can buy at any supermarket or drugstore. This book is primarily about interactive learning of basic skills. It is important, however, that the child learn to work by himself, and occasionally doing worksheets is a good way to develop motivation and self-reliance. Do not rely solely on worksheets to educate your child.

Directions:

(1) Write the alphabet in capital letters and have your child write the letters.
(2) Write the alphabet in small letters and have your child write the letters.
(3) Encourage good penmanship. Teachers have commented how penmanship skills seem to have gone away since the computer was introduced. However, penmanship is still an important basic skill.

-37-

COLOR WHEEL

> **Purpose: To learn to how colors combine.**
> **Materials Needed: Water colors, paper.**

Parent/ Teacher: Knowing colors is another basic skill. By kindergarten, the child should already know the basic colors. Explain that the colors red, blue, and yellow are primary colors.

Directions:

(1) Make the color wheel below using watercolors.
(2) Show how red and yellow make orange.
(3) Show how yellow and blue make green.
(4) Let the child experiment with colors.

Color Wheel

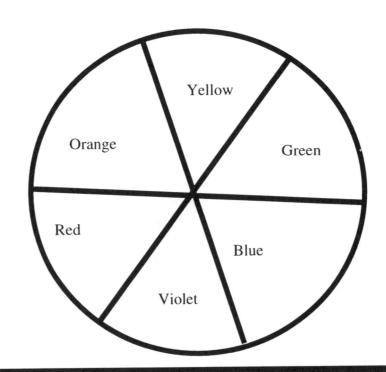

-38-

PIGS IN A BLANKET

Purpose: To learn cooking skills, how to follow directions.
Materials Needed: Hotdogs, biscuit mix, cheese, condiments.

Parent/ Teacher: Let your child do the work, following your directions. Praise him for his job.

Directions:

(1) Roll out an uncooked biscuit. Place it on a baking sheet.
(2) Put a hotdog on the buscuit. Add a slice of cheese.
(3) Fold the biscuit over the hotdog and cheese.
(4) Place in oven and bake according to the instructions on the biscuit package.
(5) Have your child help set the table.
(6) Add your favorite condiments and enjoy!

-39-

HELPING YOU THINK

**Purpose: To develop thinking and reasoning skills
and oral language.
Materials Needed: None.**

Parent/ Teacher: Read these questions to your child. Ask your child
to give reasons for their answers. Activities like this should be done
often and on a spontaneous basis because it enhances the child's ability
to think and reason.

Directions:

(1) Is soup hot or cold?
(2) If you drop a glass on the cement, what will happen?
(3) Who is older, a father or a child?
(4) Can you cross your legs?
(5) Does a turtle have wings?
(6) Is a pillow hard or soft?
(7) Can we see the wind?
(8) Do we *spill* a pan or *drop* a pan?
(9) Do we *talk* a book or *read* a book?
(10) Which is larger, a truck or a tricycle?

-40-

ROAD SIGNS & STOP LIGHTS

Purpose: To learn safety skills.
Materials Needed: Construction paper, markers.

Parent/ Teacher: Teaching your child safety skills should begin early. By kindergarten age, the child should be learning how to safely cross a street. The most important things to stress are caution, look both ways, and never assume anything.

Directions:

(1) On construction paper, make pictures of road signs and stop lights, including pedestrian crossing lights.
(2) Discuss with your child what they mean.
(3) Explain when it's safe to cross the street. Stress that even though the light may be green, it's still important to look both ways for traffic.
(4) Your child can make his own signs.
(5) Go for a walk in your neighborhood looking at signs and discuss them.
(6) Walk across a street in a congested area with predestrian lights on the stop light, and show how to do it safely.

-41-

LEARNING ABOUT SENSES

Purpose: To develop self awareness, general knowledge, and listening skills.
Materials Needed: Salt, sugar, pickles, and other flavored foods.

Parent/ Teacher: Young children's sense of taste is not yet as developed as an adult do not try foods that are overly spicy or hot.

Directions:

(1) Try tasting salt. Explain that the taste is called salty. Explain that our tongue can tell different tastes.
(2) Taste sugar and other flavors and identify them.
(3) Explore other senses: sight, hearing, smell, and touch.
(4) Ask these questions:
   What kinds of foods are salty?
   What kinds of foods are sweet?
   How do we protect our eyes?
   How does our senses protect us?
   Why is the sense of touch important?
(5) Have the child close his eyes. Let him experience touching objects and identify them. Let him listen to sounds and identify them.

-42-

OLD MACDONALD HAD A FARM

Purpose: To learn music skills and have fun.
Materials Needed: None.

Parent/ Teacher: Teach your child this familiar song and other childhood favorites. This song is often used with preschoolers to each the animal sounds, but kindergarteners love it too. Have fun with it.

Song:

Old Macdonald had a farm.
E—I—E—I—O
And on that farm he had some ducks.
E—I—E—I—O
With a quack-quack here
And a quack-quack there.
Here a quack, there a quack.
Everywhere a quack-quack.
Old Macdonald had a farm.
E—I—E—I—O

Next verses, use these animals and sounds:

pig: oink oink
cow: moo moo
dog: bow wow
chickens: peep peep
lambs: baa baa
horses: neigh neigh
cats: meow meow

-43-

SHAPES GAME

> **Purpose: To learn shapes and oral language.**
> **Materials Needed: Shapes, plus you can play**
> **music in the background ot make this more**
> **fun.**

Parent/ Teacher: Prepare objects of various shapes for playing this game. It works well with several children too.

Directions:

(1)Hold up a shape (triangle) and say, "When I hold up anything shaped like a triangle, wiggle your arms."
(2) Hold up another shape (square) and say, "When I hold up anything shaped like a square, stomp your feet."
(3) Practice with the first two shapes, then add two or three more with additional instructions (clap your hands, say "Yee ha", shake your head).
(4) Continue the game with about 5 different kinds of shapes, first doing it slowly, then increasing the speed.
(5) The game can get silly after a while, but that's part of the learning experience too!

-44-

CAN PIGS SWIM?

Purpose: To develop reasoning skills, motor
   development.
Materials Needed: None.

Parent/ Teacher: As your child grows older, this will help them develop more thinking skills. Let your imagination help with this activity. It can be silly, yet the child is learning many skills with this type of game. Learning can be fun!

Directions:

(1) Ask your child to tell your whether this statement is true or false: "Can pigs swim?"
(2) When the child answers that it's false, ask him to show you what pigs really do.
(3) Ask another question for a true or false answer. Some more questions can be: "Do fish swim?" "Do cows fly?" "Do birds walk?" "Do birds fly?" "Do turtles drive cars?" "Do horses eat hay?" "Do children ride bicycles?"

-45-

HELPING YOU THINK

Purpose: To develop thinking and reasoning skills and oral language.
Materials Needed: None.

Parent/ Teacher: Read these questions to your child. Ask your child to give reasons for their answers. Activities like this should be done often and on a spontaneous basis because it enhances the child's ability to think and reason.

Directions:

(1) Can bunnies fly?
(2) Are muffins something to wear or something to eat?
(3) Do dogs wear clothing?
(4) Are hats for hands, feet, or for the head?
(5) Is silverware really silver?
(6) Can we see sunshine?
(7) Which is larger, a tree or a bush?
(8) Since a potato has eyes, can it see?
(9) Do we stamp a *letter* or stamp our *feet*?
(10) Is a ceiling lower than a floor?

-46-

LOOK ALIKES

Purpose: To develop visual discrimination.
Materials Needed: Pencil:

Parent/ Teacher: Instruct your child to cross out the number that does not match the other ones in each box.

1 1		8 9	
1		8	
1 7		8 8	
7 7		9 9	
2		9	
7 7		3 9	
1 10		6 6	
10		6	
10 10		8 6	
3 3		4 4	
3		4	
8 3		4 9	

-47-

BUTTERFLY VOWELS

**Purpose: To learn vowels and their corresponding
  sounds.**
Materials Needed: Construction paper, crayons.

Parent/ Teacher: You make cut-outs for reinforcing any concept.
Important learning reinforcements should be put on the bulletin board or
hung in plain view in the child's learning center.

Directions:

(1) Draw a butterfly on construction paper. Inside the wings,
place one of the vowels: a, e, i, o, u.
(2) Draw one butterfly for each vowel. You can make each
one a different color to help reinforce this learning skill.
(3) Explain how vowels are important in every word we use.
Let the child name a word, and you will tell him which
vowels are in it. Emphasize correction pronunciation of each
vowel.
(4) You can make a singing game out of the sounds: a, e, i,
o, u. You can do something fun while walking around
singing the vowels. If you make it fun, the learning rein-
forcement is greater.

-48-

MAKING PUZZLES

> **Purpose: To develop reasoning skills, visual discrimination, motor development.**
> **Materials Needed: Posterboard, glue.**

Parent/ Teacher: You can use the puzzle below or make your own. To make a puzzle, find a large picture from a magazine or a catalog. Cut it out. Glue it to posterboard for more strength. Taking a black magic marker, divide the picture into large sections. Have the child cut apart the sections, then put the puzzle together. As the child gets older, you can make the sections smaller. By the time your child finishes kindergarten, he should be able to do puzzles with at least 15 pieces. By the time your child finishes kindergarten, he should be able to do puzzles with at least 15 pieces.

-49-

CIRCLED WRITING

Purpose: To develop penmanship and motor skills.
Materials Needed: Pencil and paper, crayons.

Parent/ Teacher: This is a simple way to improve your young child's penmanship. The reason it works is that she needs to concentrate on each letter and its shape.

Directions:

(1) Write the child's name in large block letters.
(2) Show the child how to go over a letter with tiny circles.
(3) The child can color in the circles with as many colors as the she wishes.
(4) Try this activity with numbers too.

-50-

BOOK ABOUT ME!

> **Purpose: To develop self-awareness, a good self concept, espressive oral language, and writing awareness.**
> **Materials Needed: Paper, crayons or markers, two sheets of construction paper, colored string.**

Parent/ Teacher: This book about your child will take some time, but it will be worth it! Follow these steps, you'll have a treasure!

Directions:

(1) Tell your child you are going to make a book about him.
(2) Gather the materials together and assemble the book. The cover should be printed by you with a self-portrait of your child.
(3) Look at baby pictures of your child. Discuss your child's size as a baby and his need for someone to feed, bathe, dress and care for him.
(4) As your child talks, write what he says. For example, "When I was a baby, I ..."
(5) Get a recent photo and let your child talk about what he can do now. Write what he says. For example, "I am 5 years-old. Now I can ..."
(6) Each day, add another page that tells about your child.

-51-

PUTTING TOYS AWAY

Purpose: To develop discipline and organization.
Materials Needed: None.

Parent/ Teacher: Organizational skills start early in children. You should be the role model for putting things in their place. If they see you do it, they will be more likely to do it. Otherwise, you will be teaching, "Do as I say, not as I do," and will have difficulty teaching them certain values and skills.

Directions:

(1) Explain that putting things away is important, and why.
(2) Show the child where things belong. You can get input from the child as to where she may want to put things.
(3) Praise the child for a job well done.
(4) Show the child where Mom puts the towels away, and Dad's workshop, where he puts his tools away.

-52-

WEATHER AND SEASONS

Purpose: To learn simple science skills.
Materials Needed: Crayons and paper, magazines.

Parent/ Teacher: Being observant of changing weather will help your child be observant of it as well. Find as many ways to explain weather and seasons as possible.

Directions:

(1) Discuss clouds, their shapes, and how they make rain. Walk in the rain, letting the children splash in the puddles (you did it too!) and show them how the water runs down the street. Explain where it goes.

(2) Talk about the sun. Walk in the sun and talk about how good it feels, how it's important to plants to have both rain and sunshine in order to be healthy, and how too much rain can make floods or too much sun can make plants dry up and cause fires.

(3) Discuss fog, frost, dew.

(4) Go walking through a gentle snowfall and discuss how snow is made. Make snow angels with them!

(5) Talk about the seasons. In the fall, show them colored leaves and explain why leaves turn colors.

(6) Using a globe, show how the earth turns in relation to the sun to make seasons. If you don't have one, use one at the library.

-53-

PLAYING STORE

> **Purpose: To develop simple math skills and to learn simple economics.**
> **Materials Needed: Paper, crayons, household items.**

Parent/ Teacher: This is an excellent activity to do with several children, but will work with one child too. Together, decide how to set up a pretend store.

Directions:

(1) Make paper money with the crayons and paper. For pretend coins, you can use buttons. Each color of button can be one value, such as red ones are nickels.

(2) You can use a toy cash register, or make one from an egg carton.

(3) Mark items to be sold in your store. Masking tape can be used to make price tags.

(4) Take turns being the customer or the storekeeper.

-54-

STORYTELLING

Purpose: To develop language arts, creativity.
Materials Needed: None.

Parent/ Teacher: Storytelling should become an activity for the whole family. Use a regular storytelling time you set aside, as well as a family reading time.

Directions:

(1) Start a story, and spend a couple of minute developing it.
(2) Then ask the child to continue it. Let him tell the story his way, without correction. Show appreciation for his input.
(3) Let everyone at storytelling hour have a chance to add to the story.
(4) Sometimes, each person can tell their own story in full, without changing from person to person.
(5) Some sessions can include grandparents, who tell stories from their childhoods. This type of family time can build bonds that last a lifetime.

-55-

GUESS WHICH ANIMAL

> **Purpose: To develop listening skills and thinking skills.**
> **Materials Needed: None.**

Parent/ Teacher: This activity can be used with plants as well as animals. When the child is pretending to be the plant or animal, it gives him a chance to develop his language skills while he's learning how to describe them. Help him with descriptive words only if he is having trouble finding the right word, or if he asks for help. This gives him a chance to search for the right word or to decide if he needs to know a new word for what he's trying to describe.

Directions:

(1) Pretend to be an animal, using sounds and movements. You can use farm animals or exotic animals. For more exotic animals, you may want to give hints, such as, "I carry my babies in my pouch."
(2) Ask your child to identify the animal.
(3) Pretend to be a plant, again using movements. This time, give hints on what kind of plant it is. "I live along the beach and have a long skinny trunk and long leaves."
(4) Give your child the opportunity to be the plant or animal.

-56-

WHAT'S NEXT

> **Purpose: To develop reasoning skills, visual discrimination.**
> **Materials Needed: None.**

Parent/ Teacher: Below, have your child tell you what figure(s) comes next in this pattern. They can draw it on paper, if you wish. You can do more of these yourself. Keep in mind that the figures should be large and easy to reproduce for a five-year-old. Pattern recognition such as this helps develop the skill necessary to recognize letter patterns in reading. It also helps develop logical thinking.

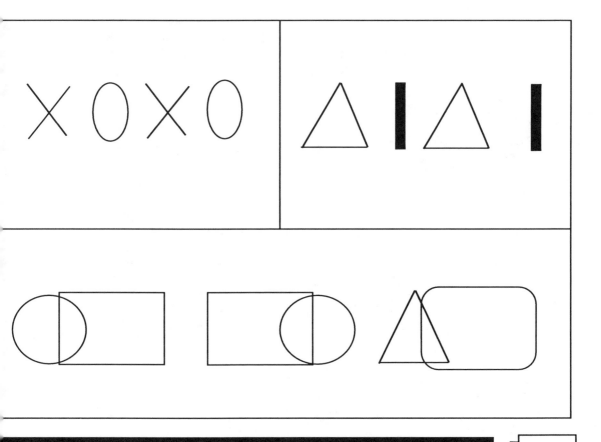

-57-

NUMBER LINE

Parent/Teacher: Help your child make a number line 1 through 10, with a space beside it for placing objects.

Directions:

(1) Beside the number 1, place one object. Beside the number 2, place two objects, etc. Have your child do the same activity with the numbers 3 and 4, and continue down the number line.

-58-

ALPHABET DISCOVERY

> **Purpose: To develop an awareness of the alphabet and sounds connected to it.**
> **Materials Needed: None.**

Parent/ Teacher: This activity can be done often, in any place that you are with your child, such as the zoo, the park, the grocery store, etc.

Directions:

(1) While in your home, go over different objects, point at them, say the word, and say the letter of the alphabet they start with. For example, point to a bed, say, "Bed. B."

(2) Have your child repeat what you say.

(3) Choose 5 or 6 objects to do this way.

(4) Then ask your child to point to something, say the word and the letter.

"Bike.B."

-59-

FAMILY READING

Purpose: To develop a love for reading.
Materials Needed: Books.

Parent/ Teacher: Reading at home is important. Designate a "Family Reading" time. For more information on how to he children learn to love to read, see Stan Wonderley's book *Success Starts Early,* also by Blue Bird Publishing.

Directions:

(1) Get your family together and agree on a time when everyone in the family will read.
(2) Agree on a place—living room or den. You must all be in the same area.
(3) Before you start, have family members select reading material.
(4) Start out with an agreed-upon time, such as 15 minutes, then extend it to 30 minutes daily. Yes, every day at the same time.
(5) The rules for reading should be agreed upon before starting the session:
> a. There will be no interruptions of family reading time. Friends and phone calls must wait.
> b. There will be no talking or interrupting another person's reading.

-60-

FIRST WE—

> **Purpose: To develop language arts, sequencing skills.**
> **Materials Needed: None.**

Parent/ Teacher: Simple activities can help your child learn to how to put things in proper sequence. This is a skill that helps the child with reading and other academic activities.

Directions:

(1) Talk about an activity, such as baking cookies.
(2) Say, "When we bake cookies, first we—" Then ask the child what you do first.
(3) Then talk about what must be done second, third, and so on.
(4) Other activities can be discussed with the same approach, such as going to the park, buying groceries, and riding a bike.
(5) If you think the child is jumping too far ahead in the sequence, say why you think something else should come first, but be sure to praise the child for her efforts.

-61-

SIMPLE GRAPHS

> **Purpose: To learn basic graph concepts.**
> **Materials Needed: Pencil and paper.**

Parent/ Teacher: This activity can be used with various items found around the house. With several children, you can count and graph things such as eye color and hair color.

Directions:

(1) Have the child go to a closet and look at the pairs of shoes.
(2) Have him count the pairs of black shoes, of brown shoes, of white shoes, and of blue shoes.
(3) Show him how to make a graph showing the numbers of each color of shoe.

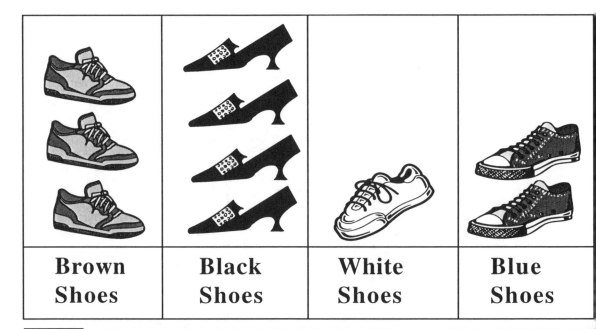

| Brown Shoes | Black Shoes | White Shoes | Blue Shoes |

-62-

MAKING A CALENDAR

Purpose: To understand time and sequence. To help the child understand organization and planning.
Materials Needed: Pencil and paper.

Parent/ Teacher: Make a calendar like the one below, only larger. Use a full sheet of 8 1/2" x 11" paper. If you make a master, you will only need to copy it each month and fill in the blanks.

Directions:

(1) While your child is watching, write the month, year, days of the week, and dates for the month you plan to start.
(2) Write activities for each weekday. Tape the calendar to your refrigerator door at your child's level.
(3) Let the child participate in the planning of activities, including learning activities.

Month_____

Sunday	Monday	Tuesday	Wednesday	Thursday	Friday	Saturday
1	2	3	4	5	6	7
8	9	10	11	12	13	14
15	16	17	18	19	20	21
22	23	24	25	26	27	28

-63-

TREASURE HUNT

> **Purpose: To learn reasoning skills, sequence skills.**
> **Materials Needed: Magazine pictures.**

Parent/ Teacher: This activity can be done outdoors on a nice day and also with several children. Older children can have written instructions instead of pictures.

Directions:

(1) Start the treasure hunt by giving the child a clue with a picture from a magazine or catalog. For instance, a picture of a telephone means that the next clue will be near or under the telephone.

(2) Explain to the child to move from clue to clue until they find a TREASURE.

-64-

CARE OF A PET

Purpose: To understand responsibility and basic science skills.
Materials Needed: Whatever is needed for taking care of a particular pet.

Parent/ Teacher: Pets are usually the first major responsibility of a child. Let them have this experience, and insist that they carry out this responsibility. If they appear to tire of a pet after awhile and start to let the responsibility fall on you, firmly remind them that caring for a pet is a responsibility for the lifetime of the pet. You are teaching values as well as basic skills.

Directions:

(1) You child will at some time want a pet. Help your child select the right kind of pet for her.

(2) Besides the obvious dog or cat pet, there are many to select from that a young child can care for: guinea pigs, rabbits, mice, gerbils, goldfish, guppies, tropical fish, turtles, lizards.

(3) Check out from the library a book on care for the pet. Read it to your child. Explain clearly what care the child is responsible for.

-65-

FLOATING & SINKING

Purpose: To learn basic science, observation.
Materials Needed: Tap water, salt water, bowl,
paper clips, corks, aluminum foil, rocks,
styrofoam cup.

Parent/ Teacher: Find additional kinds of materials that either float or sink.

Directions:

(1) Fill a bowl or plastic container with tap water.
(2) Find objects that either float or sink, such as paper clips, corks, aluminum foil, rocks, styrofoam cup.
(3) Have the child put them in water and see whether they float or sink.
(4) The most important part of this activity is observation, so help the child learn to observe.
(5) Try the activity with salt water and observe the differences.

-66-

COLOR WALK

Purpose: To develop observation skills and color recognition.
Materials Needed: None.

Parent/ Teacher: Go on a "color walk" with your child. Begin by telling your child that there's a reward at the end of the color walk (like an ice cream cone). Observe and name everything you see that is of a certain color. Green is a good color to begin with. Continue the activity with different colors. When you return home, the child may enjoy drawing and then coloring the items he saw on the walk.

-67-

FIELD TRIPS

> **Purpose: To develop a knowledge of the world around them, socialization skills, vocabulary.**
> **Materials Needed: None.**

Parent/ Teacher: Activities outside the home are very important for the child to be able to grasp what the world is about. Do these as often as possible.Besides adding to the child's general knowledge, they provide an opportunity for the child to socialize with someone outside his family. If your children are homeschooled, check into socializing opportunities with a home school support group, your church, and other community activities.

Suggestions:

      (1) Botanical Gardens.
      (2) Stable.
      (3) Office—to see what Mom or Dad do.
      (4) Library—go frequently and regularly.
      (5) Post office.
      (6) Fire Station.
      (7) Bakery.
      (8) Mechanic Shop.
      (9) Science Museum—many are interactive for children.
      (10) Parks/ Playgrounds—go frequently and regularly.
      (11) Farm.

-68-

READING HOUR AT THE LIBRARY

Purpose: To develop a love for reading.
Materials Needed: A trip to the library.

Parent/ Teacher: This is another reminder how important it is to read to your child every day. Many libraries have a special children's reading hour when someone comes in and reads to them. Parents, take your child to the library at this time. This is a good activity to join about once a week, as the child can participate in listening to the story along with other children.

-69-

BEING TOLERANT

> **Purpose: To learn how to be tolerant, vocabulary.**
> **Materials Needed: None.**

Parent/ Teacher: As with all values, tolerance is best learned by example.

Directions:

(1) Explain to the child what tolerance means: having a fair and objective attitude toward those whose opinions, practices, race or nationality differ from your own.
(2) Discuss what can be done to show tolerance. You say, "Kids were making fun of Jill because she was fat. What would you do or say?"
(3) Role-play tolerance. "I'll pretend to be Mark, who just moved here from another country. You show me what you would do or say."
(4) When situations arise involving tolerance, help your child understand the position of the other person.

-70-

BODY DRAWING

Purpose: To be able to identify body parts; to develop artistic ability and small muscle control.

Materials Needed: Butcher paper longer than your child is tall, felt tip pens and crayons or paints, tape.

Parent/ Teacher: Your child will enjoy being the central figure of this activity.

Directions:

(1) Place the butcher paper on a flat surface and tape it into place.

(2) Have your child lie on the paper, face up.

(3) Draw an outline of the child with a felt tip pen.

(4) Have your child paint or draw in the body parts, such as the nose, ears, hair, eyes, hands, and feet. Don't worry about the artistic quality!

(5) You may want to hang the finished drawing on his bedroom door. Add the child's name and the date of the drawing.

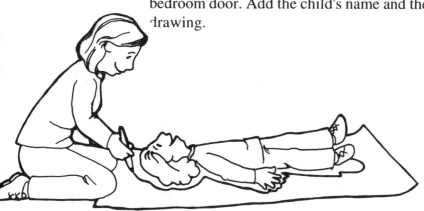

-71-

BODY CLOCK

Purpose: To learn basic time skills, motor development.
Materials Needed: Paper and pencils.

Parent/ Teacher: The child will find this a fun activity. It's also good with a group of children.

Directions:

(1) Draw a large clock on a large piece of butcher paper on the floor.
(2) Tell the child that his body will be the hands of the clock. Demonstrate it once. For 3:30, the upper part of the body will point toward the three, and the lower part of the body will point toward six.
(3) Ask the child to demonstrate several times: Noon, 6:16, 9:30, 3:00, 8:15, 7:30, and more.

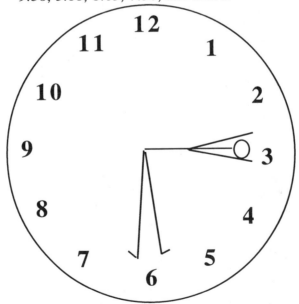

-72-

SIMPLE MEASUREMENTS

Purpose: To learn simple measurement.
Materials Needed: The self-drawing from activity
70, ruler, measuring cups, measuring spoons.

Parent/ Teacher: Find other ways to let the child learn simple measurement.

Directions:

(1) Take a ruler, and make a shape of a foot that's a foot long on a piece of paper. Have the child cut out the foot.
(2) Explain that a "foot" in measurement actually means 12 inches, not really a person's real foot.
(3) Give the paper foot to the child and ask her to measure her self drawing to see how tall she is.
(4) Write on the bottom of her drawing how tall she is and the date.

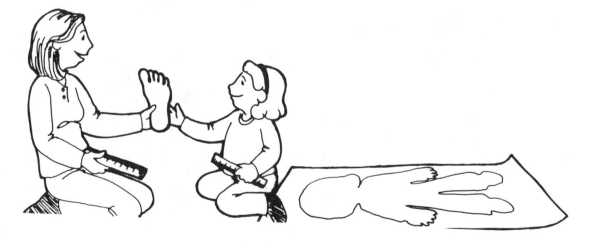

-73-

NUMBER GRAPH

> **Purpose: To learn numbers and simple charts.**
> **Materials Needed: Paper and pencils, beads,**
> **   pasta, spices, buttons, paper clips, or other**
> **   small objects, posterboard.**

Parent/ Teacher: Find numerous small household objects that the child can glue on his chart. An example is shown below.

Directions:

(1) Give the child a piece of paper with the numbers from 1 to 10 on the left side. Draw lines for a chart like below.
(2) Ask the child to glue one object beside number one, two objects besides number two, and so forth. Provide different kinds of objects he can glue: beads, pasta, spices, buttons, paper clips, etc.

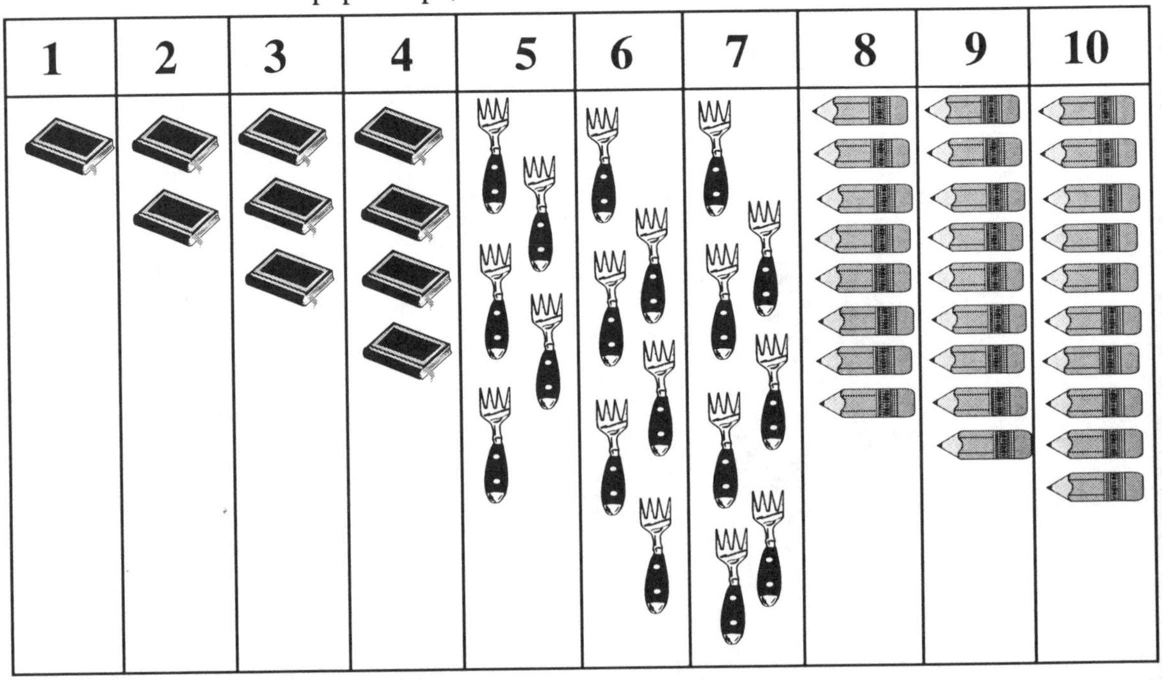

1	2	3	4	5	6	7	8	9	10

-74-

BODY RHYTHM

Purpose: To learn simple rhythm and following instructions.
Materials Needed: None.

Parent/ Teacher: After doing this with body movement, try using rhythm sticks and have your child repeat your rhythm.

Directions:

(1) Create a body rhythm, such as clap, stomp, clap, clap, stomp, stomp.

(2) Ask the child to repeat it. If it's too difficult for the child, make a simpler rhythm to start.

(3) Create more rhythms for the child to repeat. Examples:

      a. snap, clap, slap legs, snap, snap.

      b. stomp, clap, snap, clap, stomp.

      c.clap, clap, slap legs, slap legs, snap, stomp.

-75-

SAFETY RULES

Purpose: To learn basic safety.
Materials Needed: None.

Parent/ Teacher: Discuss safety whenever the topic seems appropriate, such as going to the store, going to church, while shopping.

Directions:

(1) Ask the child if they know what "safety" means. Explain it to them.
(2) Tell them there are certain safety rules you expect them to always follow. Examples:

      a. Never walk, jump or run with scissors.

      b. Never run with a stick.

      c. Walk, not run, around the pool.

      d. Never go near the pool without an adult present.

      e. Do not open the door to a stranger.

      f. Always wear a seatbelt.

      g. In case of fire, leave the building, and do not go back in until your parent says so.

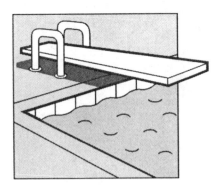

-76-

DOUGH ALPHABET

> **Purpose: To develop a recognition for the alphabet.**
> **Materials Needed: Either commercial Play-Do™ or homemade dough from flour, water, and salt.**

Parent/ Teacher: If you made homemade dough, let the child participate in that activity as well.

Directions:

(1) Prepare either dough.
(2) Show the child how to form letters of the alphabet. Show him how to make the letters to form his name.
(3) Ask him if there are other words he can make or wants to make.
(4) For homemade dough, you can bake it in the over at 350 degrees for a few minutes and the dough will harden. Then you can paint the letters, and hang them from a thread like a mobile.
(5) Do the clean up together.

-77-

THIS OLD MAN

> **Purpose: To learn a song and review body parts.**
> **Materials Needed: None.**

Parent/ Teacher: Touch the body part mentioned in the song as you sing it.

Song:

This Old Man

This old man, he played one,
He played knick knack on his thumb,
With a knick knack paddy whack,
Give a dog a bone,
This old man came rolling home.

Two ... shoe.
Three ... knee.
Four ... floor.
Five ... side.
Six ... sticks.
Seven ... up to heaven.
Eight ... on his plate.
Nine ... on his spine.
Ten ... once again.

-78-

RECYCLING

Purpose: To learn simple recycling, recognition of community.
Materials Needed: None.

Parent/ Teacher: Children should learn the three R's: Recycle, Reuse, and Reduce. They also need to know why, because this will help them realize that they are part of a larger community, and what they do affects others.

Directions:

(1) Show children your recycling bins, and show what kinds of materials go in each one. Give them the special chore of being in charge of one type of material. "You're responsible for putting the weekly newspapers in the paper recycling."
(2) Encourage them to recycle their toys and clothing. Take them to a donation drop-off with items. Show them how to shop in second-hand stores when appropriate.
(3) If you garden, show them how to compost.
(4) Show them by example. In your kindergarten program, you can use materials that you have saved instead of destroyed, like cartons, bags, berry baskets, cereal boxes. When looking at packaging, you ask the child, "What can we make out of this?" This also encourages creativity.

-79-

PEANUT BUTTER KRISPIES

Purpose: To learn basic cooking and measuring skills.
Materials Needed: Margarine, peanut butter, Rice Krispies™, marshmallows.

Parent/ Teacher: Prepare these together, letting the child do the measurements. Do the clean up together.

Ingredients:

> 1/4 C. margarine
> 1/4 C. peanut butter
> 40 regular-sized marshmallows
> 5 C. Rice Krispies™

Directions:

> (1) Melt the margarine over low heat.
> (2) Add marshmallows and melt.
> (3) Add the peanut butter and stir.
> (4) Add the Rice Krispies.
> (5) Stir all together.
> (6) Spread into buttered pan and press firmly.
> (7) Cool and cut into squares.

-80-

SWINGING

Purpose: Physical education.
Materials Needed: None.

Parent/ Teacher: If you do not have swings in your yard, go to a nearby park.

Directions:

(1) By kindergarten age, your child probably already knows how to swing. Do it with your child with zest. It's never too late to have a happy childhood!
(2) Tell your child this classic poem by Robert Louis Stevenson:

How do you like to go up in a swing,
  Up in the air so blue?
Oh, I do think it the pleasantest thing
  Ever a child can do!

Up in the air and over the wall,
  Till I can see so wide,
Rivers and trees and cattle and all
 Over the countryside—

Till I look down on the garden green,
  Down on the roof so brown—
Up in the air I go flying again,
  Up in the air and down!

-81-

A LEMONADE STAND

> **Purpose: To learn measuring and counting money.**
> **Also general knowledge and economics.**
> **Materials Needed: Table, pitcher, ice cubes, lemonade, paper cups, change, trash bag.**

Parent/ Teacher: A lemonade stand has been the first business of many multimillionaires. It's definitely a great lesson in basic economics! It's a wonderful activity for several children to do together.

Directions:

(1) Set up a table in front of your house or at the corner.
(2) Make a sign to bring in customers.
(3) Make lemonade and have cups and a trash bag available.
(4) Show your child how to make change.
(5) Clean up together at the end of the day.

-82-

MACARONI NECKLACE

> **Purpose: Art.**
> **Materials Needed: Macaronis of various shapes, paints, string or yarn.**

Parent/ Teacher: Using several shapes of macaroni will increase the interest in this project.

Directions:

(1) You can paint the macaroni before stringing into necklaces or after. Food coloring will also color the macaroni. You may want to do the coloring the day before stringing into a necklace to let the macaroni have time to dry completely.
(2) Have the child create her own necklace or bracelet by stringing the macaroni on yarn or string. She can add other objects that interest her for her jewelry.

-83-

SOMETHING BLUE

Purpose: To learn colors.
Materials Needed: None.

Parent/ Teacher: This is a wonderful activity for several children to do together.

Directions:

(1) Tell your child, "I see something blue and it's in this room. Can you guess what it is?"
(2) Your child can try to guess what it is. If there are several children, they can take turns guessing what the object is."
(3) The person who guesses will choose the next object and say something like, "I see something yellow."

-84-

EVERYDAY COUNTING

> **Purpose: Learning counting.**
> **Materials Needed: None.**

Parent/ Teacher: Practice counting whenever possible. Use objects that you are working with. When your child has mastered counting from 1 to 10, go to 20, then 50, then 100 and beyond. Here's a list of ideas.

Items to Count:

(1) Ice cubes
(2) Silverware
(3) Dishes
(4) Cookies
(5) Books
(6) Pages in a book
(7) Pieces of candy
(8) Crackers
(9) Magazines
(10) Flowers

-85-

FEELINGS

Purpose: To learn self-awareness.
Materials Needed: Magazines, scissors, glue,
   paper.

Parent/ Teacher: The purpose of this activity is to help your child become aware of her feelings.

Directions:

(1) You explain to the child that she can find pictures in the magazines that show people's feelings, such as sad, happy, silly, mad, excited. Ask her to cut out pictures that show feelings.
(2) She can glue the pictures to a sheet of paper.
(3) Underneath, you can write or help her write, the feelings that are being shown.

-86-

RAIN & WATER

Purpose: To learn simple science, vocabulary.
Materials Needed: Water, jar.

Parent/ Teacher: Set a jar outside before a rain.

Directions:

(1) Collect rain water. Explain to the child that the amount in the jar is the amount it rained, and that the weather man will tell us each day how much it has rained in the past day. Explain that it might rain 1" in your neighborhood, but a mile away, it might rain only half that amount. Tell him that an instrument that tells us how much it has rained is called a rain gauge.

(2) Talk about rain showers, how they can be heavy or light, and that a light rain is called a drizzle.

(3) Explain that after a rain, you can sometimes see a rainbow.

(4) Mark the water level of the rain you collected with a marker. Tell the child to keep an eye on the water and see what happens.

(5) When the child asks why water disappeared, you can explain evaporation.

-87-

SHAPE TRAIN

> **Purpose: To learn shapes.**
> **Materials Needed: Construction paper, scissors, crayons.**

Parent/ Teacher: The child needs to learn the names of basic shapes and be able to identify them.

Directions:

(1) Make a shape train. This is a train make of cars and engine from the basic shapes.
(2) Cut shapes from different colors of construction paper and arrange them into a train.
(3) Let your child be creative. The most important thing is that he learns the names of shapes.

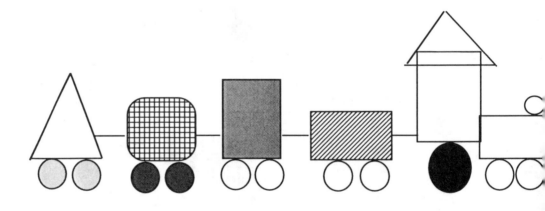

-88-

ANIMAL SOUNDS

Purpose: Learning how animals sound.
Materials Needed: Recorder and cassette.

Parent/ Teacher: You can have fun getting recording animal sounds at the zoo or on a farm.

Directions:

(1) Record various animal sounds.
(2) Play the sounds for your child.
(3) Ask your child to repeat the sounds.
(4) Record your child and play it back for him.

-89-

SEASONS

Purpose: To learn about seasons, vocabulary.
Materials Needed: Paper and pencils, magazines.

Parent/ Teacher: Explain as much as you can about each of the seasons, why they occur, and how they affect people and animals.

Directions:

(1) Divide a piece of paper into four sections, one for each season.
(2) Place a heading in each section for each season.
(3) Talk with your child about what occurs in each season. List descriptions in each section. Example:

Autumn	Winter
Falling leaves	Snow
Yellow and red leaves	Cold temperatures
Harvest time	Animals hibernate

(4) Then have your child cut pictures from magazines that represent each season and glue them onto the paper.

-90-

ONE MORE

Purpose: Learning counting and sequence.
Materials Needed: 10 objects.

Parent/ Teacher: The idea is to find out what one more means. This is a prelude to addition.

Directions:

(1) Put 10 objects into a container. This can be anything: buttons, macaroni, blocks.
(2) Ask the child to put out one object. Then ask him to put out "one more".
(3) Ask him how many objects are out.
(4) Continue to put out "one more" and ask how many.

-91-

MATCH NUMBER TO A SET

Purpose: To learn matching and number concepts.
Materials Needed: Pencil.

Parent/ Teacher: Have the child match the number to the set.

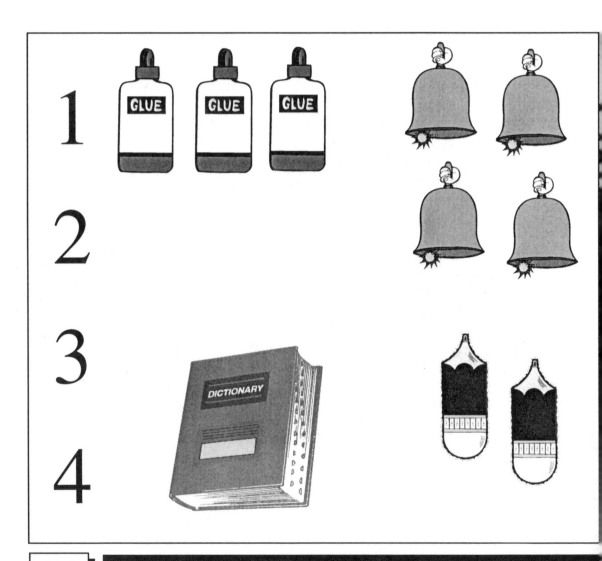

-92-

CARROT TOPS

Purpose: Simple science activity.
Materials Needed: Deep plate, carrots, water.

Parent/ Teacher: Kids always enjoy watching plants sprout from seeds. Besides this activity, try planting carrot seeds, apple seeds, or others.

Directions:

(1) Using full size carrots with green tops, cut the tops off with some carrot attached.
(2) Place on a deep plate with water.
(3) Keep watching every day for a week to see what changes happen.

-93-

DOT PATTERN

Parent/ Teacher: Have your child draw lines in the same pattern on
the right.

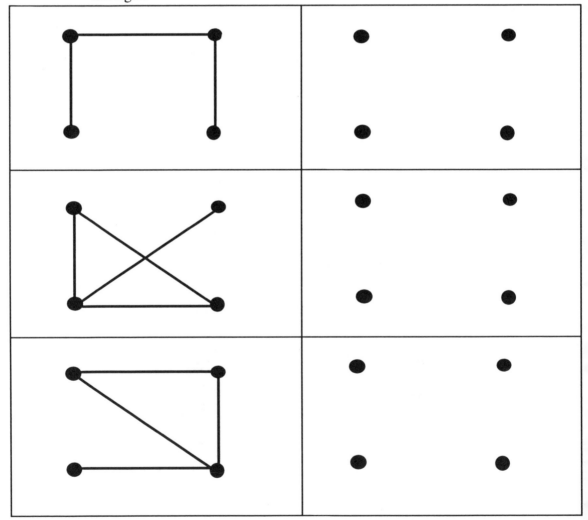

-94-

SAND LETTERS

Purpose: To learn the alphabet and simple words, to learn motor skills.
Materials Needed: Sandbox and short stick.

Parent/ Teacher: While enjoying an outdoor time together, play with your child in the sandbox. Find a short stick, and draw letters in the sand. Draw simple words, such as the child's name, and words like cat, dog, rat. Show your child how to do it, and praise her for her efforts.

-95-

JACK BE NIMBLE

> **Purpose: To learn motor skills, phsyical educa-
> tion.**
> **Materials Needed: Things to jump over.**

Parent/ Teacher: Do the poem with jumping activities.

Directions:

(1) Find small objects to jump over, such as a pillow, a cushion, a blanket.
(2) Show the child how to jump over the object, and chant the poem:

Jack be nimble, Jack be quick.
Jack jump over the candlestick.

(3) Have the child jump over the object and say the poem.
(4) Find other ways to jump, such as: jumping on one foot, jumping with a running start, jumping with two feet together.

-96-

DRESS UP

> **Purpose:** To develop large and small muscle control, to encourage creativity, and to have fun!
> **Materials Needed:** Clothing, possibly some that is too large for your child. Uniforms and costumes are extra fun for children.

Parent/ Teacher: Children—both boys and girls—love to play dress up. Let your child participate in finding items for this activity. Old uniforms and costumes are especially fun for them.

Directions:

(1) Let your child participate in selecting items for her to put on.
(2) After collecting the clothing, let your child try putting some of it on. It's best if your child does this by herself.
(3) Name the clothing items while the child is putting them on.

-97-

SHADOW TAG

Purpose: Physical education, coordination.
Materials Needed: Sunshine and shadows.

Parent/ Teacher: This works best with more than one child, although you can play too.

Directions:

(1) Have your children play shadow tag. This is played by tagging a shadow instead of the person. It works best early or late in the day when shadows are longer.
(2) On a warm day, you can add interest by using squirt guns and letting the children squirt each other's shadows. Eventually everyone will be wet, but it's great fun!

-98-

WRITING LETTERS

Purpose: Learning how to write letters.
Materials Needed: Paper and pencil.

Parent/ Teacher: Do this activity when it's time to send someone a thank-you note. That way, you are also teaching your child good manners.

Directions:

(1) Ask your child what they want to say in the letter.
(2) Show the child how a letter starts with "Dear Grandma."
(3) Write the letter for the child, letting them watch you.
(4) Show them how letters end and how envelopes are addressed and stamped.

-99-

VOCABULARY

> **Purpose: To learn new vocabulary.**
> **Materials Needed: None.**

Parent/ Teacher: Learning vocabulary will occur naturally as your child grows. Be sure to answer her questions about what words mean, and help her pronounce new words correctly.

Directions:

(1) Ocasionally, take time to purposely learn new words.
(2) You can learn new words about a particular subject, or just new words in general.
(3) Say the word, have the child repeat it, help her pronunciation, then explain what it means.
(4) Examples of words to discuss:

harvest	seasons	autumn
fizzle	activity	numeral
creative	correct	holiday
temperature	weather	senses
health	measure	rhythm
responsible	muscle	balance
directions	relatives	different

-100-

MANNERS

> **Purpose: To learn manners.**
> **Materials Needed: None.**

Parent/ Teacher: Reinforce manners whenever necessary. You can also do role-playing situations to show how things should be done.

Directions:

(1) Pretend you are on the phone calling, and your child is answering the phone. Train him to say, "Hello, this is Robert," or "Hello, Smith residence."

(2) Teach your child how to take a message if you are not available. Even though your child may not be able to write names, he should be able to write all numbers of a phone number, and ask for the person to spell his name.

(3) Teach your child to always thank someone for a gift. Thank-you notes are important to learn how to write. Tell him that even though a verbal thank-you is nice, a thank-you note should still be written.

(4) Your child should know how to say, "Excuse me," as well as "Please," and "Thank you."

(5) Teach your child that it is good hygiene as well as good manners to cover his mouth when coughing.

-101-

SIMON SAYS

> **Purpose: To practice listening skills and following directions, which are important skills for future learning.**
> **Materials Needed: None.**

Parent/ Teacher: Play Simon Says with your child to help reinforce the listening skills. You are the leader. Give directions by saying, "Simon says . . ." and finish with a direction. When playing this game, if you don't say, "Simon says . . ." first when giving a direction, the child is not supposed to do the activity. That way, you can alternate with different things to see if he is paying attention. If he mistakenly does the action when he's not supposed to, you can say, "Ooops! I didn't say Simon Says!"

Suggested Commands:

(1) Simon Says put your hand on your head.
(2) Smile.
(3) Simon Says sit down.
(4) Simon Says stand up.
(5) Touch your knee.
(6) Simon says touch your ankle.
(7) Walk around the room.
(8) Simon Says clap your hands.

-102-

ANY TIME ALPHABET

Purpose: To learn alphabet skills.
Materials Needed: Household items.

Parent/ Teacher: Find as many ways as possible, whenever possible, to teach your child how to make letters of the alphabet. If she has mastered the basic alphabet, do the same activities with simple words.

Directions:

(1) Find household objects to make into letters of the alphabet. Example: use pens or pencils to form letters.
(2) Try other objects, such as food. If you have a house rule not to play with food at the dinner table, then do this activity at a different time of day. Use dry cereal, pasta, candies, or any kind that is dry and can form letters. For example, you can break long pieces of spaghetti into letters.
(3) Use toys to form letters. Make letters from blocks.

-103-

BEING RESPONSIBLE

> **Purpose: To develop responsibility, self-control, and self-reliance.**
> **Materials Needed: A variety of household or outdoors objects already available.**

Parent/ Teacher: Teach your child to become responsible and independent by giving him small tasks to perform and expecting him to do as instructed. Do not make this a negative experience—be sure that you are doing the same tasks!

Directions:

(1) Encourage your child to hang up his clothing.
(2) Show your child where to put clothing.
(3) Encourage your child to take care of his toys and to put them away after play time.
(4) Praise your child for being neat. Don't nag—nagging will not have lasting results.

-104-

ROUGH OR SMOOTH

**Purpose: To develop tactile awareness and vo-
cabulary.**
**Materials Needed: Objects of different textures,
such as rough, smooth, bumpy, soft, hard.**

Parent/ Teacher: This is a good chance for the child to develop some
vocabulary words as well as learn the difference in how the way things
feel to touch.

Directions:

(1) Put several objects in an enclosed box. Examples of
objects to use are: feathers, seashells, balls, wood, beads,
something furry, silk, rope, rock, dried flower, bark from a
tree, cotton ball.
(2) Have the child put her hand in the box and find an object.
with her eyes closed, she can take the object out and feel it
with both hands.
(3) Ask her to describe how it feels. Encourage words such
as rough, smooth, bumpy, hard, soft, cold, wet.
(4) Ask her if she can tell what the object is by feeling it. Let
her open her eyes and see it.
(5) Try another object.

-105-

ROPE MOVEMENTS

Purpose: Physical education, coordination.
Materials Needed: 18 inch piece of rope.

Parent/ Teacher: Rope activities teach an interesting group of skills.

Directions:

(1) Give your child a short piece of rope about 18" long.
(2) Ask your child to stretch the rope in front of himself. See how many ways he can move it.
(3) Ask him to move it behind him, in front of himself, up and down, around.
(4) Can your child hold the rope and jump over it?
(5) Can he crawl over the rope one leg at a time?

-106-

KEEPING A JOURNAL

> **Purpose:** To understand that writing is "talking on paper" and that what someone writes, someone else can read.
>
> **Materials Needed:** Blank book—can be purchased at bookstores.

Parent/ Teacher: After a trip or an experience, write about it in your child's journal.

Directions:

(1) Encourage your child to tell about an experience, such as a visit to the zoo.

(2) Write down what your child says. (Printing is best.)

(3) Read back what your child said and you wrote.

(4) Leave room at the bottom of the page for illustrations. Make this a pleasant activity so that the child will want to continue it.

-107-

BEFORE AND AFTER

Purpose: To learn sequence skills, vocabulary.
Materials Needed: Camera (optional).

Parent/ Teacher: You can take pictures of the process you are doing so that later you can discuss the sequence.

Directions:

(1) Pick an activity that has several steps so that the child can learn a sequence. Examples: making orange juice, making a salad, making cookies.
(2) Do the activity together, making note of the order in which things are done.
(3) Use words like: before, after, first, next, then, finally, first, second, third, fourth, etc.

-108-

PAPER CHAINS

Purpose: To learn simple measurement, motor skills.
Materials Needed: Construction paper, tape.

Parent/ Teacher: You can use the paper chains to decorate the child's room after the activity is done. Your child can use several different colors to use on the chain if she wishes.

Directions:

(1) Have your child make a paper chain by cutting strips of construction paper and taping them in a chain.
(2) When the chain is at least two foot long, have the child use the chain to measure objects. For instance, you can say, "See how long the spoon is. Oh, it's 4 links long."
(3) Then encourage the child to find things to measure with the paper chain.
(4) She can even make the chain as tall as she is. You will need to help her count the number of links in a chain that long.

-109-

BEING COMPASSIONATE

> **Purpose: Social skills.**
> **Materials Needed: None.**

Parent/ Teacher: Teaching compassion for people who are different may be easier than you think. The best way is by example. Children have a natural empathy. All you need to do is give them an opportunity to do good for others.

Directions:

(1) Do something for a shut-in person. Plan a meal and prepare it with your child. The two of you can deliver the meal to them.

(2) Donate your time to help deliver food boxes to those in need. Be sure to discuss why people may be poor and talk to your child about how to help.

(3) Be sure you tell your children that they should never talk to poor, homeless or unfortunate people in a way that would hurt their feelings.

-110-

SHAPES

Purpose: To learn shapes.
Materials Needed: Crayons.

Parent/ Teacher: Read your child the directions below and have them complete the activity.

I am a square.
Color me orange.

I am a circle.
Color me red.

I am a triangle.
Color me yellow.

-111-

LETTER MATCH

Purpose: To learn sounds and how to match.
Materials Needed: Pencil.

Parent/ Teacher: Have your child draw a line from the letter to the word that starts with the letter.

-112-

COLOR THE CAR

**Purpose: To learn how to follow directions, small
motor skills.**
Materials Needed: Crayons.

Parent/ Teacher: Tell your child to color the car red, but its wheels
should be colored brown and the windows blue. This is a lesson in
following directions, not in creativity, so see that they complete the
activity the way that you request.

-113-

LEARNING OPPOSITES

Purpose: To develop vocabulary meaning.
Materials Needed: Magazines

Parent/ Teacher: Discuss the seasons and how it is warm in the summer and cold in the winter. Talk about ice being cold and boiling water being hot. Discuss how night is opposite of day. Then let the children find opposites in a magazine and cut them out and explain to how how they are opposites.

-114-

RHYMING WORDS

Purpose: To develop auditory discrimination.
Materials Needed: None.

Parent/ Teacher: Say the following lists of words and have your child repeat them. Listening to and saying rhyming words develops auditory discrimination, which is good for reading. Also, read to your child the book *Rhythmic Phonics* from Blue Bird Publishing, which contains silly poems in a format that teaches phonics. When your child shows an interest in starting to read, an excellent learn-to-read book is *Dr. Christman's Learn-to-Read Book* by Blue Bird Publishing, which also uses phonics.

cat	pan	night
bat	man	right
rat	fan	fight
mat	ran	light
fat	can	might
car	lick	boy
star	kick	toy
far	sick	joy

-115-

MOTOR SKILLS

Purpose: Physical education, coordination.
Materials Needed: None.

Parent/ Teacher: Children of kindergarten age enjoy these activities and they are good activities for developing their physical skills. Join in if you are physically able to do so.

Directions:

(1) Encourage your child to do summersaults, headstands, and cartwheels. Praise his efforts.
(2) Show him how to do a bridge if you are able. Ask him to do one.
(3) These physical activities can be done in water as well. If your child enjoys the water, ask him to do headstands and rolls in the water.
(4) Jump rope is another good physical activity for this age.

-116-

HELPING YOU THINK

Purpose: To learn how to think, vocabulary.
Materials Needed: None.

Parent/ Teacher: Read questions to your child. If she does not know the answers, lead her to discover them. Make this a fun time.

Directions:

(1) Could you walk with four legs?
(2) Can a dog walk on two legs? Why or why not?
(3) What is the difference between a farm and a garden?
(4) What is a triangle? A rectangle? An oval?
(5) How often do we need to buy groceries?
(6) What is the difference between a truck and a bus?
(7) What is language? What language(s) do we speak?
(8) Why does the grocery store have cereal in boxes but apples are not in boxes?
(9) What are nails made of? Feathers? Shells?
(10) What happens when we eat food?

-117-

THE ONE BETWEEN

> Purpose: To develop directionality and vocabu-
>   lary.
> Materials Needed: Pencil.

Parent/ Teacher: Have your child circle the one between. You should demonstrate with real objects; have your child stand between two chairs, two books, etc.

-118-

THE UNITED STATES

Purpose: To learn social studies, vocabulary.
Materials Needed: Globe (optional).

Parent/ Teacher: The object is to teach the child basic citizenship.

Directions:

(1) Tell your child that his country is the United States.
(2) Show your child a map of the U.S. or point to it on the globe.
(3) You can explain that his state is _____ and point to it on the map.
(4) Tell him that he is a citizen, which means that he is a member of this country.
(5) Tell him things he can to do be a good citizen.

-119-

A TRIP TO THE GROCERY STORE

Purpose: To develop visual discrimnation, expressive oral language, and classifying skills.
Materials Needed: None.

Parent/ Teacher: Prepare to take your child along shopping for groceries by first letting him cut out pictures from grocery ads and paste them on a paper list for what you plan to buy at the store.

Directions:

(1) Talk to your child about what foods will be served at dinner.
(2) Let your child help choose the foods that are eaten. Have him cut out pictures from the ads and paste them on paper.
(3) When you go to the store, let the child find the items on the list.
(4) Talk about vegetables in the produce section and what you will look for in the canned goods section.
(5) Discuss each of the child's items after you arrive home, whether they need to be refrigerated, and how they will be prepared for the meal.

-120-

PAPER BAG MASKS

Purpose: Art, motor skills.
Materials Needed: Large paper bags, crayons or markers, construction paper, pipe cleaners, yarn, scissors.

Parent/ Teacher: Do this with several children if possible.

Directions:

(1) Cut two holes out of a large paper bag for the eyes.
(2) Decorate the mask with bits of construction paper, pipe cleaners, yarn, ribbon, or whatever.
(3) Let the children put on their masks and create a play.

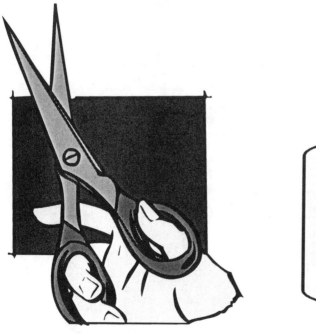

-121-

COUNT THE STARS

Purpose: **To develop visual discrimination, vocabulary, and counting skills.**
Materials Needed: **None.**

Parent/ Teacher: There is a number of skills that are acquired by doing this activity.

Directions:

(1) Have the child count the number of stars in the triangle.
(2) Have the child count the number of stars in the circle, then count the number of stars in the square.
(3) Ask him to count the number of stars in the area which is part of the circle <u>and</u> part of the square.
(4) Ask him to count the number of stars in the area which is part of the circle <u>and</u> part of the triangle.
(5) Your child may need help with this activity, but be patient because there is a lot of skill learning going on.

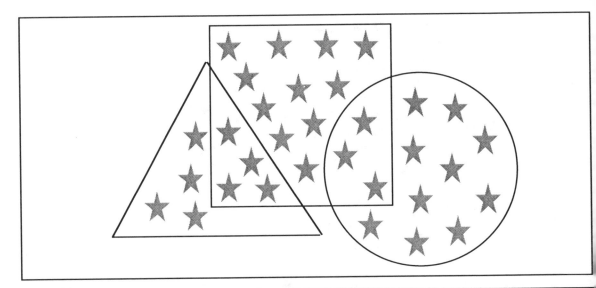

-122-

FINGER PAINTING

Purpose: To learn how to express emotions, art, creativity.

Materials Needed: Water based paints, paper.

Parent/ Teacher: Let your child be as expressive as she wishes. Your child will learn that she can express emotions through art.

Directions:

(1) Spread out newspapers to an easy clean-up before doing this activity.

(2) Make a face of a person on the paper, and make an expression for happy, sad, funny, angry, silly, afraid. Tell your child what you have done.

(3) Ask your child to make faces that show feelings.

(4) Have her describe to you the emotions on the people she draws.

-123-

HEALTH COLLAGE

Purpose: Learning how to stay healthy, vocabulary.
Materials Needed: Magazines, catalogs, scissors.

Parent/ Teacher: Teaching cleanliness, exercise, and good nutrition are as important as academics.

Directions:

(1) Write on a piece of poster board, "Things that keep us healthy."
(2) Discuss with your child good health habits: brushing teeth, washing hands, exercise, good nutrition, vaccinations, proper rest, vitamins.
(3) Ask your child to find pictures in magazines and catalogs that of things that keep us healthy or people doing things that are healthy.
(4) Glue or tape the pictures on the poster board in a collage.

Things That Keep Us Healthy

-124-

TREES ARE IMPORTANT

Purpose: To learn about nature and science.
Materials Needed: A walk in the trees.

Parent/ Teacher: This activity can be a discussion of the environment and its importance to us.

Directions:

(1) Go for a walk where there are trees. An especially good place to talk about trees is in the old forests, especially in places that have giant redwoods or other forests that have never been harvested.
(2) Talk to your child about how important trees are to the world and the health of the planet, how trees create the oxygen we breathe and clean the air.
(3) Hug a tree. Look at its bark, its leaves, its branches.
(4) Discuss ways we can be good to trees. Talk about recycling paper and reusing things when possible.

-125-

GIANT BUBBLES

> **Purpose: Science, vocabulary.**
> **Materials Needed: Bubble solution, either commercial or homemade, cans or six-pack holders or berry baskets.**

Parent/ Teacher: You can teach science concepts while having a great time. Kids always love this activity.

Directions:

(1) You can use commercial bubble solution or make your own by mixing 8 tablespoons liquid dishwashing soap with 1 quart water. Adding a tablespoon of glyercine will make better bubbles (available at pharmacies).

(2) Make bubbles with cans that have both ends gone, or berry baskets or six-pack rings.

(3) Ask the child to look at the bubbles and see how many colors he sees. Why do the bubbles float away? Why do they pop? What do you see in the bubbles?

(4) When the child sees himself upside down in the bubble, explain that the bubble acts like a lens and shows upside down pictures. You can talk about other kinds of lenses.

-126-

SOCK PUPPETS

> **Purpose:** Art, creativity, motor skills.
> **Materials Needed:** Large sock, stuffing, rubber band, scraps of material, yarn, buttons.

Parent/ Teacher: Let your child be as expressive as she wishes. Your child will learn that she can express emotions through puppets.

Directions:

(1) Take an old sock and stuff it with newspaper, old material, or rags.
(2) Tie the end with a rubber band.
(3) The child can decorate the face with material, yarn, buttons, pipe cleaners, construction paper, or markers.
(4) You can add strings to the top of the puppet's head to make it move. Let the child experiment with it.
(5) You can also remove the stuffing and let the child put her hand inside and make the puppet come alive.

-127-

CLUES

Purpose: Learning how to give clues and how to guess from clues, auditory discrimination, reasoning.
Materials Needed: None.

Parent/ Teacher: This activity can teach reasoning skills as well as help develop speech. This is a good activity to do in the car.

Directions:

(1) Begin by giving a clue, "I am thinking of something that is soft and pink and cuddly. Can you guess what it is?"
(2) The child guesses, and gives the next clue.
(3) Clues can be about anything in the room. Examples:
"Something wood and hard and you sit on it."
(chair)
"Something round and it ticks and it tells time."
(clock)

-128-

MIRRORING

Purpose: To learn how to express emotions, self-awareness.
Materials Needed: None.

Parent/ Teacher: This is a form of "monkey see, monkey do."

Directions:

(1) Sit facing your child.
(2) Tell your child that you are going to show a "feeling" on your face, that you are going to express an emotion. You want her to guess what it is and imitate it.
(3) Show the feeling, let the child imitate it, and do another and another.
(4) Let your child lead the activity.

-129-

DRAWING TO MUSIC

Purpose: Art, creativity, music appreciation.
Materials Needed: Paper, crayons.

Parent/ Teacher: Music not only enhances our lives, but it gives us outlets for creativity and emotions.

Directions:

(1) Play music.
(2) Let your child draw something original.
(3) Play different kinds of music: classical, rock, jazz, etc.
(4) Afterward, discuss your child's creations with him. Talk about different kinds of music affect us differently and how it may have affected what he drew.

-130-

YOGURT FRUIT COCKTAIL

Purpose: Basic kitchen skills, manual dexterity.
Materials Needed: Fruit cocktail, grapes, yogurt.

Parent/ Teacher: Be sure to do the clean up together.

Directions:

(1) Let your child slice grapes in half and add them to fruit cocktail.
(2) Let your child mix the fruit cocktail with yogurt.
(3) Ask your child to help set the table for a snack.
(4) Enjoy the yogurt fruit cocktail together.

-131-

EGG CARTON JEWELRY BOX

> **Purpose: Art, creativity, manual dexterity.**
> **Materials Needed: Egg cartons, paints, decorations.**

Parent/ Teacher: Your child can do this project for herself or as a gift. Cardboard egg cartons work better than styrofoam ones.

Directions:

(1) Paint the outside of the egg carton and let dry.
(2) Paint the inside of the egg carton and let dry.
(3) Decorate the egg carton. Ideas: construction paper, pipe cleaners, ribbon, yarn, pictures from magazines.

-132-

MUSIC POSTER

> **Purpose:** Music appreciation. vocabulary.
> **Materials Needed:** Poster board, magazines, cata-
>   logs, glue, tape.

Parent/ Teacher: This activity is to help your child learn about instrument and learn some music vocabulary.

Directions:

(1) Write on the top of the poster board, "Things that make
music."
(2) Talk with your child about different kinds of instruments, both traditional and nontraditional. Discuss how
body parts can be instruments as well: hands can clap, feet
can stomp, fingers can snap, mouths can whistle.
(3) Have your child cut pictures from magazines and catalogs of things that make music. Glue them on the poster.
(4) Discuss musical terms: instruments, rhythm, beat,
melody, tune, composer, songwriter, piano, guitar, cello,
violin, clarinet, saxophone.

Things That Make Music

-133-

WEIGHT

**Purpose: Learning what things weigh, simple science,
comparisons.
Materials Needed: Scale.**

Parent/ Teacher: Compare many items of different weights with this
activity so that child develops a concept of heavy and light.

Directions:

(1) Get a bathroom scale.
(2) Weigh your child. Tell him his weight.
(3) Ask him to weigh another object. Ask him if it weighs
more or less than him. He may not know which numbers are
bigger than others, so you may need to help him.
(4) Pick an object in the room. Tell the child you are going to
weigh it, but first he should hold it and guess its weight.
Then weigh it.
(5) After several objects, your child will start grasping the
concept of weight, which is heavy and which is light.

-134-

VISIT A PAINT STORE

Purpose: To learn about colors, career awareness.
Materials Needed: None.

Parent/ Teacher: This activity can teach the child about colors and hues as well as learn about how people earn a living.

Directions:

(1) Take your child to a paint store.
(2) Look at the color samples and discuss things likes hues, shades.
(3) Tell your child that the people who work there sell paint to people who paint their houses, their rooms, and other things that need painting. That is how they earn their living.
(4) Let your child ask the store clerk a couple of questions.

-135-

MORE OR LESS

Purpose: Basic math, vocabulary.
Materials Needed: Pencil.

Parent/ Teacher: Explain to your child the concepts of "more" and "less." Then have your child follow the directions below.

1.Color the group that has more.

1.Color the group that has less.

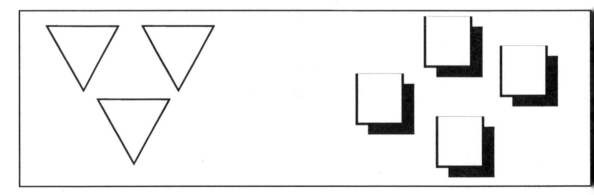

-136-

ROW, ROW, ROW YOUR BOAT

**Purpose: Music appreciation. auditory discrimination.
Materials Needed: None.**

Parent/ Teacher: This familiar tune is fun for kids and a good family song for travelling in the car. When your child has mastered singing it, you can try doing it in rounds. That is, one person has finished the first line, the second person starts the song. It creates a very melodic effect. Keep in mind that doing rounds might be challenging for your kindergartener, so be patient.

Directions:

Row, Row, Row Your Boat

**Row, row, row your boat
Gently down the stream.
Merrily merrily merrily
Life is but a dream.**

-137-

HONESTY

**Purpose: Learning about honesty, values training.
Materials Needed: None.**

Parent/ Teacher: Again, the best way to teach values is by example. The family is the best and most important teacher of honesty.

Directions:

(1) Tell your child what the word honesty means: not lying, cheating, stealing, or taking unfair advantage, being honorable, truthful, trustworthy, sincere and genuine.

(2) Discuss situations where honesty is shown. "Honesty is a very important value because if your friend can't trust you, you won't have any friends." "Mary was honest when she told Mom that she broke the dish. She said she would replace it with her babysitting money."

(3) Role-play situations where honesty is displayed. "I'll be the store clerk and I'm giving you back too much change. What would you do?"

(4) Praise your child when he is honest.

(5) Above all, set a good example. Drive the speed limit, and tell your child it's important. Give back store clerks change if they give you too much. Keep your business dealings fair. These are the things by which your child will learn honesty.

-138-

ESTIMATION

Purpose: To learn how to estimate, vocabulary.
Materials Needed: Ruler, yard stick.

Parent/ Teacher: Learning how to estimate is a good reasoning activity, and also related to math skills.

Directions:

(1) Using a rule and a yardstick, go over what "one foot" "two feet" "one yard" "two yards" means.
(2) Measure some objects in the room.
(3) Then pick an object, and have the child estimate what that object will measure. Explain to the child that estimating means taking your best educated guess.
(4) Then measure the object to see how close the estimation was.
(5) Keep doing this activity and your child's estimations will get closer and closer.

-139-

ALPHABET BOX

Purpose: Learning the alphabet and corresponding sounds.
Materials Needed: Boxes.

Parent/ Teacher: Your child will be learning the alphabet and its corresponding sounds. This activity encourages that skill.

Directions:

(1) Take several boxes and label the ends with letters of the alphabet. Write a capital letter and the corresponding small letter beside it, such as "Ww".

(2) You don't need to do the whole alphabet. By now, you should know which letters the child has mastered, and which ones she is having some difficulty with. I suggest doing this activity with the letters that need more work.

(3) Ask the child to find objects that start with that letter and put them in the box. For example, in the box marked "Kk" she could put keys.

(4) She can also cut pictures from magazines and catalogs that show objects that start with that letter.

-140-

RIDE A BICYCLE

Purpose: Motor skills.
Materials Needed: Bike, with or without training wheels.

Parent/ Teacher: Your child's motor skills are still developing. At this age, a child should learn to ride a bike with or without training wheels.

Directions:

(1) Help your child learn to ride a bike. This is often one of the moments a child will remember forever, and it's important that you are there.
(2) Discuss bike safety, where to ride, where not to ride, how to signal, always wear a helmet, be courteous and cautious.

-141-

BALLOONS

> **Purpose:** To improve motor skills, to learn math concepts.
>
> **Materials Needed: Balloons.**

Parent/ Teacher: Balloons can be used to teach many skills, including math, ABC's, and motor skills.

Directions:

(1) Give your child a balloon.
(2) Ask your child to tap the balloon in the air and see if he can hit the balloon straight up in the air with his head and do it again.
(3) Ask your child to hit the balloon up with his knees; his elbows; his feet.
(4) Ask your child to tap the balloon up, turn around while it's in the air, and tap it again as he comes around.
(5) Ask your child to tap the balloon up and clap (while counting out loud) 3 times while it's up in the air; then 4 times; then 5 times; then 6 times. See how many times he can clap while it's in the air.

(6) Ask your child to tap the balloon up and recite the alphabet while it's up in the air. The next time, he continues from where he left off until he finished the entire alphabet.

-142-

TRIANGLES

Purpose: To learn shapes and sizes.
Materials Needed: Triangles of various sizes.

Parent/ Teacher: Your child needs to learn the concepts of smallest, next, and largest.

Directions:

(1) Cut out triangles of various sizes.
(2) Shuffle them up, then have the child place them in order of smallest to largest.
(3) While the child is ordering the triangles, say things like, "Which is smallest?" "Which is next?" "And next?" "And largest?" That way she will hear the terms you want her to learn.
(4) Shuffle them up and do the reverse: have the child order them from largest to smallest.

-143-

BRUSHING TEETH

Purpose: To learn hygience concepts.
Materials Needed: Toothbrush and toothpaste.

Parent/ Teacher: By this age, your child has been brushing her teeth for years, and should be able to brush her own teeth unassisted. Now is a good time to talk about the importance of why brushing teeth is important.

Directions:

(1) After your child has brushed her teeth, give her a few reasons why brushing teeth is important: It keeps our teeth and gums healthy. If our teeth were not healthy, they would fall out and we couldn't chew our food. Brushing teeth also makes our breath fresh, which makes it more pleasant for people around us.
(2) Take paper and pencil, and draw a big healthy smile. Tell her this is a smile from a person who brushes.
(3) Ask her to draw her own smile.
(4) Ask her to find smiles in magazines that are nice and put them on the bulletin board.

-144-

REPEAT MY STORY

> **Purpose: Listening skills, auditory discrimination.**
> **Materials Needed: None.**

Parent/ Teacher: Practice this activity often because it helps the child learn to remember what he has heard. Memory skills can be developed, and this activity helps for auditory memory.

Directions:

(1) Tell a story that is about three simple sentences long.
(2) Ask your child to repeat it.
(3) Tell another one the same length and ask your child to repeat it.
(4) Start lengthening the story and asking your child to repeat it. Make the stories silly so this activity is fun.
(5) Continue as long as the child is enjoying this activity, but not so long that they become frustrated.

-145-

LEARNING HELPFULNESS

Purpose: To learn how to be helpful.
Materials Needed: None.

Parent/ Teacher: Helpfulness should be learned by example, but these activities will help the child understand what helpfulness is.

Directions:

(1) Explain to your child what helpfulness means: giving aid or assistance to others.
(2) Tell him that when someone says, "Help!" or is in pain or danger or asks for assistance is the most important time to try to be helpful. Explain that we all feel better when we help someone, and they feel better too.
(3) Ask your child if they know of something they can do to be helpful. They may say something like, "Being helpful means helping someone do something they can't do."
(4) Role-play. Tell your child that you are in the grocery store and you have your arms full of groceries and are at the door. What should he do?

-146-

ICE, WATER, AND BOILING

Purpose: Simple science concepts.
Materials Needed: Ice, pan.

Parent/ Teacher: Point out to your child the different properties of water at different termperatures.

Directions:

(1) Let your child fill ice cube trays with water and place them in the freezer.
(2) After the ice is frozen, show the child what has happened to the water. Ask if they know why this has happened. Explain that the cold temperature of the freezer has changed the water into ice.
(3) Place the ice into a shallow pan and place on the stove. Turn on the heat and let the ice cube melt as the child watches. Then bring the water to a boil.
(4) Again, explain that the temperature change has brought about the change in the water.

-147-

HOW TO TRAVEL

Purpose: To learn about how people move from place to place, social studies, vocabulary.
Materials Needed: Poster board, magazines, crayons or markers.

Parent/ Teacher: This activity can teach your child vocabulary as well as how people travel.

Directions:

(1) Make a poster with the title "How People Travel."
(2) Draw a truck, a bus, an airplane, a boat, a bike, and a person (pedestrian) at the top.
(3) Talk about the different kinds of transportation. Your child can learn the words: pedestrian, transportation, subway, streetcar, monorail.
(4) Let your child find pictures in magazines that show different kinds of transportation and put them on the poster under each category.

Transportation: How People Travel

-148-

LEFT AND RIGHT

Purpose: To learn left from right.
Materials Needed: None.

Parent/ Teacher: There are many adults who do not know their left from their right, so teach this to your child early. Make sure that they master this concept.

Directions:

(1) "Simon Says" can be played with all commands using left and right:

"Simon Says" put your left hand on your right arm.
Put your left foot on your right foot.
"Simon Says" wiggle your right ear with your left hand.

(2) Play "Hokey Pokey" with commands for left and right body parts. Do this for left hand, right elbow, left shoulder, right ear, left hip, right knee, etc. Play this around a circle with as many children as you wish.

You put your left hand in.
You put your left hand out.
You put your left hand in
And you shake it all about.
You do the Hokey Pokey
And you turn yourself around.
That's what it's all about.

-149-

GIVING DIRECTIONS

Purpose: To learn how to give directions, sequence skills, left and right, vocabulary.
Materials Needed: None.

Parent/ Teacher: Many people cannot give clear directions. Let your children start practicing this early so that they learn how to be precise.

Directions:

(1) Ask child how to get to some place fairly simple, like the backyard. Request that she use the words "left" and "right" in her directions.
(2) Let her explain it in her own words, but gently help if needed. Tell her this is how we give directions to someone.
(3) Then give directions to her for something a bit more complicated, like how to get to the corner store.
(4) After asking her if she understands what it means to give directions, ask her to give directions some place.

-150-

FAMILIAR RHYMES

> **Purpose: Language arts.**
> **Materials Needed: None.**

Parent/ Teacher: Get a book of familiar rhymes. Your child can learn to recite them by memory. This activity helps children reproduce sentence patterns.

Rhymes:

Jack and Jill

Jack and Jill went up a hill
To fetch a pail of water.
Jack fell down
And broke his crown
And Jill came tumbling after.

Mary Had A Little Lamb

Mary had a little lamb
Its fleece was white as snow
And everywhere that Mary went
The lamb was sure to go.

-151-

MUSCLES, BONES, AND ORGANS

> **Purpose:** To understand the human body, simple science, health, vocabulary.
> **Materials Needed:** Paper, pencil, crayons.

Parent/ Teacher: You can enhance this activity by showing your child pictures of the human body's skeletal system and muscular system.

Directions:

(1) Tell your child what a muscle is and what it does. Ask him where he has a muscle. Ask him where another muscle is.

(2) Tell him that there are things inside our body that we can't see on the outside but they help us do the things we do. These are muscles, bones, and organs.

(3) Explain what bones are, how they are the structure of our body. Show him where certain bones are, and name them, like the skull.

(4) Explain what organs are and what they do for us. Talk about the stomach, the lungs, and the heart. Tell your child that these organs are protected by our skeleton and our muscles.

(5) Your child can draw pictures of muscles, bones, and organs.

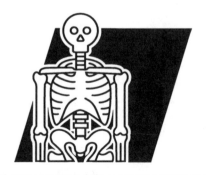

-152-

BIRDS & DUCKS

> **Purpose:** Simple science, vocabulary.
> **Materials Needed:** Something to feed birds.

Parent/ Teacher: There's a lot that can be learned by watching birds and ducks. Point out the ones that are more aggressive or passive, or how a female carefully guards her young.

Directions:

(1) Find a place to sit and watch the birds with your child. If possible, find a place with a pond that also has ducks. Take food to feed the birds and the ducks.
(2) Show your child how to break up the food into small pieces for the birds.
(3) Name the kinds of birds and ducks that come to feed. Show her which ones are female and which ones are male.
(4) Talk about how the birds find food on the ground and ducks find food in the water. Tell them about beaks, webbed feet, wings.
(5) Describe how a bird makes a nest. Find one in a tree and point to it and tell them how in the spring there are eggs in the nest. Ask your child never to disturb a bird's nest if she finds one in a tree or on the ground.

-153-

DAYS OF THE WEEK

Purpose: To learn days of the week, vocabulary.
Materials Needed: Pencil.

Parent/ Teacher: You can use the list of days of the week below or make your own. Name the days of the week in order, and have your child repeat them. Let your child draw what they might want to do on each particular day.

Sunday
Monday
Tuesday
Wednesday
Thursday
Friday
Saturday

-154-

BOTANICAL GARDEN

> **Purpose:** Learning about plants, basic science, vocabulary.
> **Materials Needed:** None.

Parent/ Teacher: Take your child to visit a botanical garden or an arboretum.

Directions:

(1) Point out plants and their names. Help your child learn which plants are common in your area.

(2) Explain how plants make food from water, sunlight, and the nutrients in the soil.

(3) Tell your child what happens to the plants in different seasons.

(4) Tell about plants in other parts of the world: the rainforest, the desert, the far north. Explain that plants are different in other areas because the climate is different.

-155-

SELF-RELIANCE

Purpose: To learn self-reliance.
Materials Needed: None.

Parent/ Teacher: It's been said that you should not do for a child what she can do for herself. That teaches self-reliance. If we do too much for our children, we take away their chance to learn how to do it for themselves.

Directions:

(1) Tell your child what it means to be self-reliant, and that sometimes it's important to learn how to do certain things by herself, and that at other times, it's important to learn how to do certain things with other people (cooperation).
(2) Give your child activities that she is expected to do on her own, without assistance. These should be things that she has already mastered the skills for, yet have some challenge to them so that she can have the satisfaction of achieving something new on her own.

-156-

BREAD DOUGH CLAY

Purpose: Art, motor skills.
Materials Needed: Clay, either commercial or
   homemade.

Parent/ Teacher: You can use commercial clay or make some using
bread. This activity can be messy, but the kids love it. Make sure they
help with the clean up.

Directions:

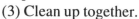

(1) Homemade recipe: several slices of bread (broken up into
pieces), 2-3 T. white glue, a couple of drops of lemon juice.
Mix together. This mixture, after scupted into objects, will
dry in 2-3 days.
(2) Encourage your child to make a scupture from clay.
Allow them freedom of creativity. Don't tell them what they
have to make, and don't interfere unless they ask for your
help.
(3) Clean up together.

-157-

SMELLING

Purpose: To understand the senses.
Materials Needed: Things to smell.

Parent/ Teacher: Suggestions for things to smell are: cinnamon, vanilla, cloves, perfume, coffee, tea, pepper, mint, chocolate, lemon, orange, onions.

Directions:

(1) Gather items to smell. Place a small amout each material in a container.
(2) Don't tell your child what the items are. This activity can be done with or without a blindfold.
(3) Ask your child to smell one item. See if she can guess what the item is.
(4) For the items that are edible, the child can have a taste after guessing what the item is.

-158-

PUDDING PAINT

Purpose: Art, motor skills.
Materials Needed: Pudding. wax paper.

Parent/ Teacher: Make sure the child helps with the clean up.

Directions:

(1) Make instant pudding. If you make a couple of different flavors, like chocolate and vanilla, or vanilla and pistachio, the child can work with a couple of different colors. You can save some of it for a treat for after the activity.
(2) Tell your child that this time the pudding is paint, and they can finger paint with it.
(3) Spread wax paper to paint on.
(4) Clean up together.

-159-

PLASTER HANDPRINT

Purpose: To develop self-recognition, art.
Materials Needed: Plaster, shallow container.

Parent/ Teacher: This is an item which the child can look at and say, "This is me!"

Directions:

(1) Mix Plaster of Paris according to the directions on the package. This can be found in a craft shop.
(2) Pour the plaster mix into a shallow container, such as a pie tin.
(3) Request that your child place his hand in the plaster, but not covering the whole hand. That will leave an impression of his hand in the plaster.
(4) Let the plaster set until it hardens.
(5) Your child can paint the plaster after it's hard. He can put his name below the handprint.

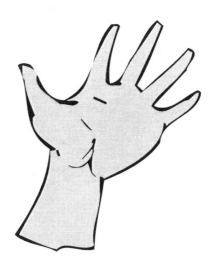

-160-

BALANCE AND COORDINATION

Purpose: Motor skills.
Materials Needed: None.

Parent/ Teacher: Your kindergartener is developing his sense of balance and coordination. You can help with these activities.

Directions:

(1) For balance, try walking on a plank that's 4" to 5" wide.
(2) Practice skipping. Skipping while singing a tune is even better.
(3) Simple dances teach coordination. Your kindergartener may want to learn something popular, like a country line dance. Try an easy one first so they can master it.
(4) Hop on one foot. Hop on the other foot. Hop on both feet. Have hop relay races. Sack races are good for this and are a good family activity.
(5) Run in place.

-161-

THE PRESIDENT AND THE WHITE HOUSE

Purpose: Social studies, sense of citizenship.
Materials Needed: Newspaper.

Parent/ Teacher: Encourage respect for our President and the leaders of our country. When children hear disparaging remarks about our leaders, what they learn is that authority figures do not deserve respect. You can explain to a child that you don't always agree with our leaders, but you respect them for the tough job they have to do.

Directions:

(1) Tell your child that the leader of our nation is the President and he/ she lives in a city called Washington DC in a place called the White House.
(2) Show the child a recent newspaper article with a picture of the President and/or the President's spouse. Tell your child the important work that the President must do.
(3) Let your child draw a picture of the President and/or the White House.
(4) Discuss with your child the qualities it takes to be a leader, and that any child with leadership qualities can grow up to be President.
(5) Tell your child that many of the same leadership qualities it takes to be President are good qualities for leaders in other areas.

-162-

IF YOU COULD

Purpose: Imagination, creativity.
Materials Needed: Paper, crayons or markers.

Parent/ Teacher: Not all daydreaming is bad or a waste of time. Some of our greatest inventions were discovered by people who were considered to be "daydreamers". Allow some time for creative thought.

Directions:

(1) Ask your child, "If you could create a new way for people to travel, what would it be?"
(2) Allow your child time to ponder this question.
(3) Let your child draw his creation on paper.
(4) Other If-You-Could questions for creative thinking might be, "If you could make a new animal, what would it be?" "If you could make a new kind of house, what would it be?"
(5) Your child may want to create with blocks or other types of materials rather than on paper.

-163-

ON THE MOON

> **Purpose:** To understand simple science, creativity, vocabulary.
> **Materials Needed: None.**

Parent/ Teacher: This activity can be enhanced by showing pictures or videos of astronauts landing on the moon.

Directions:

(1) Tell your child about space travel that humans have achieved. Talk about flight to the moon.

(2) Discuss the kind of transportation it would take to get to the moon and how long it would take and how it would affect people.

(3) Your child will have difficulty understanding the concept of the distance from the earth to the moon, but you can try to put it in an analogy that he will understand. One way of showing the distance is to use rubber balls. Explain that one rubber ball represents the earth, and a small one represents the moon. Hold the smaller one a long distance away from the larger one, and explain that it's a long long way from the earth to the moon.

-164-

DEVILED EGGS

Purpose: Cooking skills, motor skills.
Materials Needed: Hard-boiled eggs, mayonnaise,
salt, pepper, small bowl, serving plate.

Parent/ Teacher: You can use commercial clay or make some using bread. This activity can be messy, but the kids love it. Make sure they help with the clean up.

Directions:

(1) Let your child help crack and peel the shells.
(2) Show your child how to cut the eggs in half and remove the yolk. Let him do some of the eggs himself.
(4) Ask the child to mash the yolks. Tell him how much mayonnaise, salt, pepper, and other ingredients to add. Optional ingredients are: low-fat ranch dressing instead of mayonnaise, relish for flavoring instead of salt and pepper.
(5) Ask the child to spoon the filling on the egg whites.
(6) Place the eggs on a serving tray.
(7) Clean up together.

-165-

THE SUN

> **Purpose:** Simple science, to understand heat.
> **Materials Needed:** Household items.

Parent/ Teacher: Suggestions for things to use are: light and dark T-shirts, gloves, cooking utensils and bowls.

Directions:

(1) Gather items to place outside in the sun on a warm sunny day. Use items that are dark and light, plastic and metal.
(2) Place these items in the sun for half an hour.
(3) With the child, feel the items. Discuss why the dark ones are warmer than the lighter ones. (Be careful with metal items so no one is burnt.)
(4) Explain that dark items absorb the heat and light ones reflect it. Tell the child that's why white shirts are more comfortable on a sunny warm day than dark shirts.

-166-

RESPECT

Purpose: To teach values, respect and self-respect.
Materials Needed: None.

Parent/ Teacher: Your child will learn respect by watching you. Be sure you are respectful to others and to yourself.

Directions:

(1) Explain to the child what the word respect means. Tell her that respect means respect for yourself and respect for others. Self-respect is taking care of yourself, physically, mentally, socially, spiritually. Respect for others means treating others as we wish to be treated.

(2) Respect for authority means obeying the law. If we feel a law is wrong, we must respectfully try to change it.

(3) It's never too early to explain to a child that her body is to be respected, by herself and by others. If someone does something or tries to do something that she feels is not respectful to her body, she has the right to say no!

-167-

WHAT IF?

Purpose: Thinking and reasoning skills. creativity.
Materials Needed: None.

Parent/ Teacher: Ask your child the following "What If?" questions. These questions encourage thinking and reasoning skills and creativity.

Questions:

(1) What if all animals could talk?
(2) What if there were no cars?
(3) What if everyone looked alike?
(4) What if dogs could fly?
(5) What if all food tasted like pudding?
(6) What if there were no TV?
(7) What if there were no adults?

-168-

VOCABULARY

Purpose: Vocabulary.
Materials Needed: None.

Parent/ Teacher: Write the following words on poster board and place on the bulletin board. Pronounce them for your child and the explain their meanings. Review them throughout the week.

Words:

encourage	review
repeat	skills
measure	pyramid
reminder	volunteer
opposites	similar

-169-

READING REMINDER

Purpose: To encourage reading.
Materials Needed: Books.

Parent/ Teacher: This is a reminder to read to your child everyday. The most effective way to encourage your child be a good reader is to read to her everyday from her very first days. Are you reading to your child?

-170-

COMPUTERS & YOUR CHILD

> **Purpose: To start computer skills.**
> **Materials Needed: Computer.**

Parent/ Teacher: Young children learn computer skills very quickly. Many four-year-olds are already adept on the computer. Since computer skills are becoming more and more necessary in today's world, and will be even more important in our children's world, encourage your child to learn how to use the computer. There are numerous educational CD-ROMs available for young children. Also, if you want to teach your child how to use the Internet, there are programs available to screen their access to objectionable materials.

Suggested Software:
   (1) *A Little Kidmusic*™, for kids 3-13, teaches music notation, pitches, how to play a tune, rhythm with sounds of piano, guitar, organ, and voices. Available for any Macintosh using System 6, $75. ArsNova, call toll-free 1-800-445-4866.
   (2) *Sheila Rae, the Brave,* has won more than 60 awards. It contains 20 interactive pages and helps kids ages 3-7 with word recognition, vocabulary, and spatial reasoning. *ABC by Dr. Seuss*, a children's book brought to life. Available from Broderbund Software in most stores or call (415) 382-4400.
   (3) *Ready for School*™ ($79.95) with alphabet and letter recognition, numbers and counting, sorting and matching. *ABC's Featuring the Jungle Jukebox*™ ($49.95) where students learn the alphabet while singing along. *1-2-3's Featuring the Counting Critters*™ ($49.95) teaches kids their numbers as they ride the bus to different places. Available from Davidson and Associates, Inc., in most stores or call customer service toll-free at 1-800-545-7677.
   (4) *Marvin the Moose*, volumes I to IV, for ages 3-8, ($29.95) teaches moral values and approaches such subjects as peer pressure, handicaps, and teamwork. Available from Milliken Publishing Company, call toll-free 1-800-325-4136.

-171-

THE NEWS

> **Purpose:** To understand the date, social studies.
> **Materials Needed:** Poster board, construction paper, markers, tacks.

Parent/ Teacher: This will teach your children some basic words.

Directions:

(1) Make a poster board like below.
(2) You and your child can write the days of the week on construction paper. The child can tack the day of the week on the poster.
(3) Your child can make pictures of different kinds of weather: sunny, rainy, cloudy; and you can write the words beside it. The child can tack the weather on the poster.
(4) The child can clip and article from the newspaper and put on the poster.

The News

Today is _____.
The weather is _____.
Current news today is _____.

-172-

SEEDS

Purpose: Simple science.
Materials Needed: Carrot seeds, lemon, apple,
   orange, watermelon, soil, pot.

Parent/ Teacher: Spring is a good time to try this. You can explain that spring is a time of new growth, and the time farmers plant their crops and people plant their gardens.

Directions:

(1) Cut open an apple, a lemon, an orange, and a watermelon.
(2) Look at the seeds. Tell your child that seeds are necessary for growing new plants. An apple seed is potentially an apple tree. A lemon seed could grow into a lemon tree.
(3) Tell your child that certain things are necessary for growing a new plant: a seed, soil, water, and sunlight.
(4) Ask your child if he would like to grow his own plant. (Of course he would!)
(5) Plant carrot seeds shallowly in soil in a small pot. Give it a little water and place it in the sun.
(6) Let the child check the pot daily to see when the seed starts growing.

 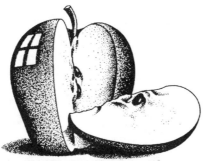 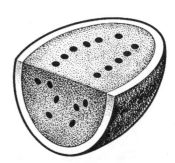

-173-

BIG—BIGGER—BIGGEST

Purpose: To understand comparisons.
Materials Needed: Poster board, magazines.

Parent/ Teacher: You can do this activity with big—bigger—biggest, small—smaller—smallest, tall—taller—tallest, or any number of words.

Directions:

(1) Write the words on a poster board in order.
(2) Let your child cut out objects that show the comparisons.

Big	**Bigger**	**Biggest**

Small	**Smaller**	**Smallest**

-174-

POPSICLE STICKS FUN

> **Purpose: To learn shapes, patterns.**
> **Materials Needed: Clean, dry popsicle sticks.**

Parent/ Teacher: Have the child make common shapes with the popsicle sticks, such as squares and triangles. Then have the child use the sticks to make the patterns below.

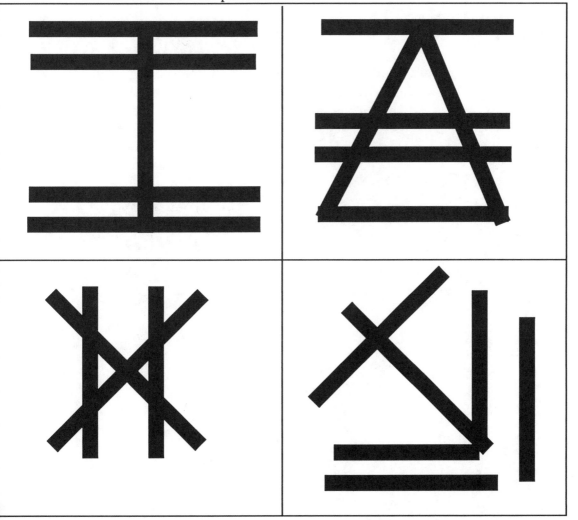

-175-

ROCK SORTING

Purpose: To learn how to sort and classify.
Materials Needed: Rocks, stones, shells.

Parent/ Teacher: This is a good activity for outdoors, such as at the park or at the beach.

Directions:

(1) Your child will be naturally interested in rocks and shells. When you're at the park or the beach, encourage your child to gather a pile of either rocks or shells.
(2) Ask your child to sort the shells according to color.
(3) Then your child can sort them according to size or shape.

-176-

READING MUSIC

> **Purpose: To understand that music can be written.**
> **Materials Needed: Poster board, markers.**

Parent/ Teacher: Make some musical notes on poster board using a marker and hang this on the bulletin board or refrigerator. This will teach the child that there is a relationship between music we hear and written music. Understanding this relationship also reinforces the child's understanding that there is a relationship between the words we hear and written language.

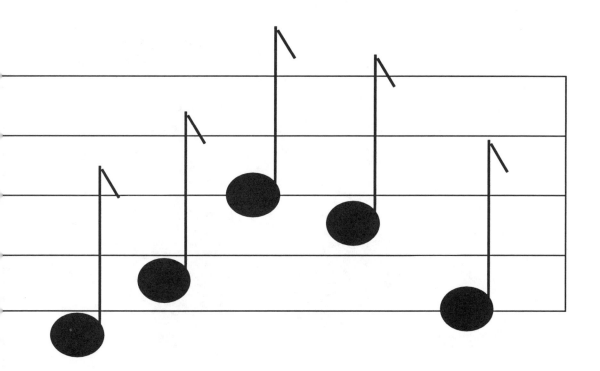

-177-

FRIENDS

Purpose: To understand the importance of friends and social skills.
Materials Needed: None.

Parent/ Teacher: Social skills, such as understanding the importance of family and friends, start early.

Directions:

(1) Talk about friends with your child. Explain the importance of friendship.
(2) Ask your child if he understands the qualities that make a person a good friend.
(3) Stress the importance of trust, honesty, loyalty. A good friend sticks by a person even when things are difficult.
(4) Name friends of the family, and ask him who his friends are.

-178-

MAKE A NEWSPAPER

> **Purpose: Language arts, social studies.**
> **Materials Needed: Legal-size paper or larger, markers, magazines or photos.**

Parent/ Teacher: Make a newspaper with your child.

Directions:

(1) Use larger paper than normal to make a newspaper, and fold it. The best size to use is 11" x 17", but legal size will do as well.

(2) Decide on a name for the newspaper. "The Smith Family News" or the like will do.

(3) Create a headline. A good idea is to make the headline about one of the child's accomplishments. "Ruthie Learns to Ride a Bike!" "Bill Catches a Fish!" "Sarah Goes to Africa!"

(4) Let your child dictate the story and you write it for her.

(5) Add photos about the event or clippings from magazines to illustrate the newspaper.

-179-

WHEN I'M ANGRY OR UPSET

Purpose: Social skills.
Materials Needed: None.

Parent/ Teacher: Teaching your child appropriate ways to release and express anger or being upset is important.

Directions:

(1) Talk to your child about what it feels like to be angry or upset. Ask your child to tell your about a time when he was upset and what he did. Ask him if he thought it was a good way to deal with it.

(2) Give your child ideas on appropriate ways to release anger: exercise, drawing, talking about it.

(3) Emphasize that strong feelings happen to people, and it's important to find a way to express or release those feelings without hurting themselves or others.

-180-

ALIKE AND NOT ALIKE

Purpose: To learn when items are similar, math skills.
Materials Needed: Pencil.

Parent/ Teacher: Read your child the directions below.

Circle the group where all the things are alike.

 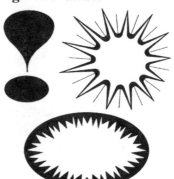

Circle the group where the things are not alike.

-181-

POST OFFICE

Purpose: Social studies.
Materials Needed: None.

Parent/ Teacher: Take your child to the post office with a letter she has written.

Directions:

(1) Explain that the post office is where letters and packages are mailed to that they go to people in other cities.
(2) Show your child what stamps look like and where they are put on letters.
(3) Give your child some money and let her buy a stamp to mail a letter she has written.
(4) Let your child put the stamp on the letter and put it in the mail slot.

-182-

POTATO PRINTS

Purpose: Art, creativity.
Materials Needed: Potatos, tempera paint, knife,
   shallow containers, paper.

Parent/ Teacher: When your child is older, she can do her own
carving on potatos. For your kindergarten child, have her make the
design she wants, and you carve it for her.

Directions:

(1) Cut potatos in half. Put tempera paint in shallow containers.
(2) Tell your child that you are going to make designs on the
potato that she can use to stamp designs on paper. Ask what
kind of design she would like on the potato. She can even
draw it on paper so you can see it.
(3) Carve the potato in the design she wants.
(4) The child can either dip the potato in the paint, or brush
paint on the potato. Then stamp the potato on the paper.
(5) With two or three potato designs, she can create a pattern
on paper.

-183-

COLORS POSTER

Purpose: To recognize different colors.
Materials Needed: Poster board, magazines.

Parent/ Teacher: This kind of activity can be done for many other learning skills, such as shapes, numbers, letters, or simple words.

Directions:

(1) Make a poster that says "Colors".
(2) Put the name of several colors on it. If your child is having trouble recognizing a particular color, make sure to put it on this poster. child should already know the basic colors, so choose more exotic colors.
(3) Have your child cut pictures from magazines or catalogs that are the chosen colors and tape them to the poster.
(4) Hang the poster in a visible place, and let the child add to it when he wants to.

COLORS

Navy blue   Turquoise   Pink   Beige   Silver   Gold

-184-

HOW MUCH IS THAT DOGGIE IN THE WINDOW?

Purpose: Music.
Materials Needed: None.

Parent/ Teacher: Sing the following popular tune with your child.

Song:

How Much is That Doggie in the Window?

How much is that doggie in the window?
The one with the waggly tail.
How much is that doggie in the window?
I do hope that doggie's for sale.

-185-

QUILT SHAPES

Purpose: To recognize different shapes and patterns.

Materials Needed: None.

Parent/ Teacher: Have your child draw lines to match the patterns below. You can easily make more patterns with construction paper or pieces of cloth for your child to work with.

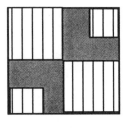
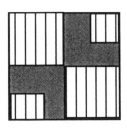
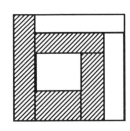
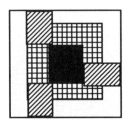
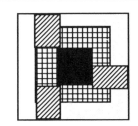
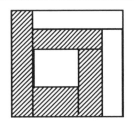

-186-

SWIMMING

> **Purpose: Muscle development, coordination.**
> **Materials Needed: Pool or beach.**

Parent/ Teacher: Swimming involves many muscles and teaches coordination and timing. Teach your child to swim at a young age. Do it gently and do not force them to do more than she is ready for. You want this to be a pleasurable experience.

Directions:

(1) First let your child become accustomed to shallow water and playing in it. The beach is a good place for this because kids love to play in the sand near the water's edge. They will become accustomed to having water around them and it will not frighten them.
(2) Then play at the water's edge, things like tag, chasing games but don't go too deep yet.
(3) It should be a natural progression that your child is eager to start learning a little more about swimming. Then teach your child how to hold her breath and go under water.
(4) Make a game of holding breath, first for the count of 5, then 10, then 15. Praise your child for her efforts.
(5) Then you can start teaching dog paddling and kicking.
(6) When your child has mastered the basics, she will be ready to learn the basic American crawl. If you haven't learned it yet, it's time for you to do it too!

-187-

GOING TO THE BEACH

> **Purpose: To learn how to plan, organizational skills.**
> **Materials Needed: Picnic and beach items.**

Parent/ Teacher: So you're going to the beach! Great! Let your child help plan what to take along. This teaches organizational and planning skills.

Directions:

(1) Tell your child about plans to go to the beach a day or two ahead of time. Tell him that you are going to take a picnic and you need to plan everything ahead of time and you would appreciate his help.

(2) Let him help you make a grocery list for the items needed for the beach, and he can help find these items at the grocery store.

(3) Let him help make sandwiches, snacks, and ice cubes.

(4) When it's time to start packing, ask him what needs to be packed, and how. That way, he can learn how to pack the cooler, which items need to be kept cool, and help decide which other items need to go along.

(5) Don't forget the sunscreen!

-190-

PEACE STARTS WITH ME

> **Purpose: To learn social skills.**
> **Materials Needed: Paper, crayons or markers.**

Parent/ Teacher: Your child should understand that he is important, and that one person can make a difference in the world.

Directions:

      (1) Let your child make a poster like the one below.
      (2) Talk about peace and what it means.
      (3) Discuss how peace begins with one person.

I can help with peace today.
I will work and play coopeartively.

PEACE STARTS WITH ME.

-191-

NUMBER FLASH CARDS

Purpose: To develop number-numeral awareness.
Materials Needed: Heavy paper, markers.

Parent/ Teacher: Drills are important for memory skills. One thing you can do is make flash cards for either numbers or alphabet.

Directions:

(1) Make flash cards like the one below for numbers 1-20.

4	2
four	**two**

-192-

WHAT HAPPENED TO ME TODAY?

Purpose: To develop oral communication.
Materials Needed: None.

Parent/ Teacher: Your child likes to have a chance to talk about himself and be the center of attention. When this is going on, help him keep things in a logical sequence, but don't interrupt him. Show respect for his story just as you would expect respect for you while you're telling your story.

Directions:

(1) Tell your child that you are going to take turns telling each other what happened to you today.

(2) Tell the details of your day in sequence, but not talking too long.

(3) Tell your child it's his turn. Encourage him to tell about his day in sequence, with enough details to understand what happened. You and say things like, "And then?"

-193-

PLAYING CONCENTRATION

> **Purpose: To develop visual memory, to learn to follow rules.**
> **Materials Needed: Playing cards.**

Parent/ Teacher: Let your child win at this as often as you do, so he will gain confidence in his skills.

Directions:

(1) Get 8 or 10 playing cards. Name each card and show them to your child.

(2) Then turn the cards upside down on a table or the floor.

(3) Take turns pointing to a card and guessing what it is. If the child guesses correctly, he picks up the card and takes another turn. If the guess is wrong, the card is placed face down again.

(4) Another version of this is to have several pairs of cards. Place them face down. One person turns over two cards. If the cards match, the player keeps the cards and takes another turn.

-194-

STRAWS

Purpose: To learn size, ordering, measuring.
Materials Needed: Straws or pipe cleaners, ruler.

Parent/ Teacher: Putting items in order of size teaches sequence skills plus simple measurement. These skills help with reading and also with math.

Directions:

(1) Cut straws or pipe cleaners into different lengths.
(2) Ask your child to arrange the straws into order from smallest to largest.
(3) Then mix them up and ask the child to arrange them from tallest to shortest.
(4) Give the child a ruler and ask her to measure the straws in inches.

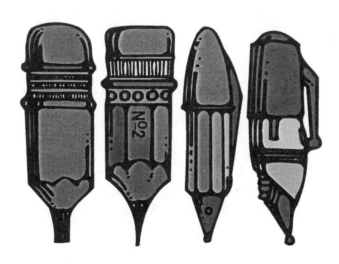

-195-

LIGHT AND ELECTRICITY

> **Purpose: To learn simple science, vocabulary.**
> **Materials Needed: Light bulb.**

Parent/ Teacher: Teaching safety about electricity should accompany this activity.

Directions:

(1) Show a new light bulb to your child. Point to the filament and explain that's the part of the light bulb that creates light.

(2) Let your child know that electricity is used to make light bulbs work.

(3) Talk about conserving electricity by turning lights off when not in use. Tell how conserving electricity helps the environment.

(4) Make shadows using the light from the light bulb and explain that even though it is not sunlight, it can still create shadows.

-196-

COURAGE

> **Purpose: To learn social skills and values.**
> **Materials Needed: None.**

Parent/ Teacher: Your child should understand that courage doesn't mean turning into a bully, but rather standing up for what it right.

Directions:

(1) Discuss courage with your child. Ask him if he thinks a bully has courage. Tell him that bullies are just plain mean, and it takes more courage to stand up to meanness.

(2) Let your child understand that a courageous person might still feel fear, but will stand up for what is right in spite of his fear. Standing up for what is right will help overcome fear.

(3) Role-play courage. Make up a situation in which the child would have to confront an obstacle and show courage. "Jaime, you're walking home with your friends, and thunder starts in the distance, and it starts to rain really hard. Your friend Rita starts to cry and wants to stop walking. What would you do?"

(4) Praise your child for showing courage.

Having courage is not the same as having no fear. Courage is being able to recognize that I have fear and still go forward.

I will have courage today.

-197-

STARS

Purpose: To develop motor skills, learn shapes.
Materials Needed: Paper, markers.

Parent/ Teacher: Drawing stars can be complicated for young children, so be patient while teaching them how to draw stars.

Directions:

(1) Using heavy paper and markers, teach your child how to draw stars.
(2) Let your child practice this drawing. It's fairly complex for her, so let her work at it.
(3) Color in the stars together.
(4) Put them on the ceiling in your child's room.

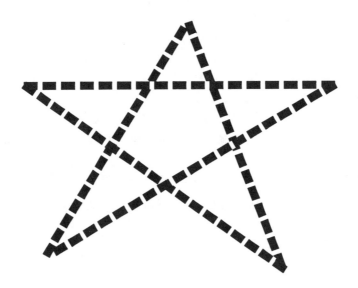

-198-

MAKE THIS BETTER

> **Purpose:** To develop critical thinking skills.
> **Materials Needed:** Paper, crayons or markers.

Parent/ Teacher: Your child should show a comprehension for some details in this activity.

Directions:

(1) Draw a house like the one below.
(2) Ask your child to add things to the drawing that make it better, and color it.

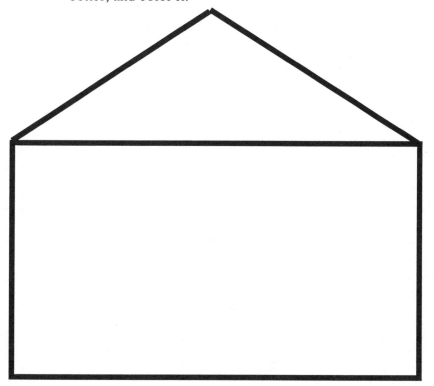

-199-

WHAT HAPPENS AND WHY?

Purpose: To develop logic.
Materials Needed: Crayons.

Parent/ Teacher: Your child should understand the relationship between things happening. You can use a larger sheet of paper for this.

Directions:

(1) Tell your child, "It had been raining. Then the sun came out and then—" Let your child draw what happens.
(2) Tell your child, "Flowers were growing nicely. Then hail came and—" Let your child draw what happens.

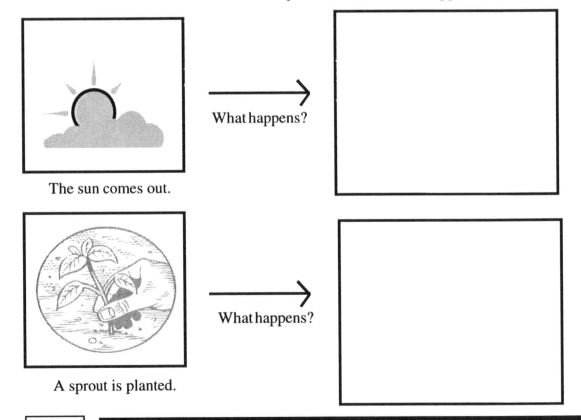

The sun comes out.   What happens?

A sprout is planted.   What happens?

-200-

DIGITAL CLOCKS

Purpose: To learn how to tell time.
Materials Needed: Digital clock, paper, crayons.

Parent/ Teacher: Although we traditionally have taught time using round clocks with numbers and hands, many clocks are now digital. As parents, we must teach our children how to read both kinds of clocks, and show the relationship between time on each one.

Directions:

(1) Draw a traditional kind of clock on paper or a paper plate. Using popsicle sticks or tooth picks, mark the time.
(2) Tell your child that there are two kinds of clocks: the regular old-fashioned kind, and the modern digital kind. Show the time on both kinds of clocks.
(3) Explain that one kind of clock lets us figure out that time it is by where the hands are, and the other one gives us numbers.

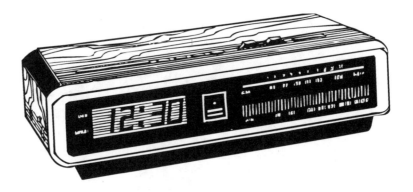

-201-

THREE-LEGGED RACE

Purpose: To show cooperation, to develop muscles and coordination.
Materials Needed: Potato sack or wide piece of cloth.

Parent/ Teacher: You need at least four people to do this, so try this activity at a picnic or event with other people around. Be sure to do it on grass so if you fall down it's soft.

Directions:

(1) Organize the group for a three-legged race. Pair off.
(2) Each team will need either a potato sack or a wide piece of cloth. With the cloth, tie one of your legs together with one of your partner's leg. That makes three legs between the two of you.
(3) Let each team practice for a minute or two before the race.
(4) Do some three-legged races. It's loads of fun but it also teaches cooperation ("How are we going to get there from here? Oh, first we use the outer legs, then the inner one!").

-202-

WHAT DO YOU WANT TO BE?

> **Purpose: To develop critical thinking skills.**
> **Materials Needed: Paper bags, crayons or markers.**

Parent/ Teacher: Your child's ideas on what she wants to be when she grows up will probably change over the years. Give her a chance to explore lots of ideas. When very young, most children will want to do what Mommy or Daddy does. Later, they may explore other ideas. You may want them to go into a certain field, but remember, it's their choice. The most important thing you can do is give them encouragement for whatever their choice is. Your support matters to them.

Directions:

(1) Ask your child, "What do you want to be when you grow up?"
(2) After she answers, ask for more details. "What does an architect do? Why would you choose that profession?"
(3) You can talk about what you wanted to be when you were young, and how you ended up doing what you're doing now.
(4). Say to her, "Let's make a masks about what people do for a living."
(5) Let her choose what profession to make the masks of.
(6) Make masks from paper bags, markers and crayons. Add decorations from construction paper and yarn.

-203-

LAUGHTER LIGHTENS THE WORLD

> **Purpose: To develop an understanding of laughter.**
> **Materials Needed: Poster board, crayons.**

Parent/ Teacher: This is good activity to do after a comedy program that's caused both of you to laugh a lot.

Directions:

(1) After something that has caused both of you to laugh hard, talk about the benefits of laughter. Tell how laughter helps people feel better, even if they had been feeling bad.
(2) Explain that laughter is beneficial for health too, and our body responds positively to laughter, even when ill.
(3) Ask your child if he remembers a time when he was feeling upset or sad, but laughing made him feel better.
(4) Draw a poster like the one below and let the child decorate it.

Laughter helps lighten the world.
I will be lighthearted and laugh today.

-204-

MAKING MUSIC WITH GLASSES & SPOONS

> **Purpose: To develop an interest in music.**
> **Materials Needed: Glasses, spoons, water.**

Parent/ Teacher: This activity will show your child different musical sounds from common household items.

Directions:

(1) Take several water glasses and fill them at different levels with water. If you have different kinds of glasses, use a variety of types.

(2) Let your child take a spoon and tap the glasses gently to make musical sounds.

(3) Ask the child to try tapping the glasses above the water and below. See what kinds of sounds are made at each level.

(4) Try making rhythmic sound with spoons on a hard surface.

(5) Join the child in composing a tune with the musical glasses and rhythmic spoons.

-205-

THEM BONES

Purpose: To learn about bones.
Materials Needed: None.

Parent/ Teacher: Point to the different bones and name them with your child.

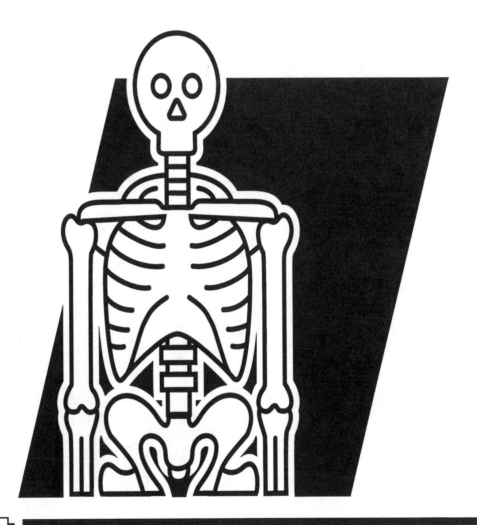

-206-

PARTS & WHOLES

Purpose: To understand the relationship between parts and wholes.
Materials Needed: Depends on activity chosen.

Parent/ Teacher: This activity will help your child understand the relationship between parts and wholes. This is preliminary to a child understanding fractions and other mathematical or scientific relationships.

Directions:

(1) Order a pizza. When it comes, talk about how the pizza is all one piece when it comes out of the oven (whole) but then it is cut into smaller pieces. Ask the child if he thinks that the pizza can become all one piece again.

(2) When working on something with parts, let the child participate, or at least watch. Talk to the child about the parts that make up the whole thing.

(3) For example, when changing the battery on a digital clock, show the child the back of the clock, where the battery goes, what it does, and how it contributes to the clock as a whole.

(4) For activities involving early fraction understanding, divide fruit into sections and talk about the sections, calling by the proper fraction: "We'll take this apple and divide it in half. Then we'll divide each half again, and we'll have fourths."

-207-

PAPER AIRPLANES

Purpose: To learn about air and wind.
Materials Needed: Sheet of paper.

Parent/ Teacher: Try different aircraft designs. Some work better than others.

Directions:

(1) Ask your child to throw a piece of paper toward you and see what happens.
(2) Then ask him to wad the paper into a ball and throw it toward you. Does it go any farther?
(3) Make a paper airplane. Let your child make one too.
(4) Throw the paper airplanes around the house and talk about their movements.
(5) Go outside and launch them into the breeze and talk about air and wind and how the air movement will keep the planes in the air.
(6) Have airplane contests. Play airport.
(6) To add stability to your paper airplanes, you can add a lightweight round object to the rear of your airplane, such as a piece of cardboard paper towel tube about 1/2" wide.

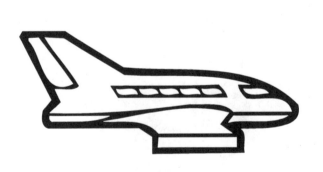

-208-

GELATIN POPCORN BALLS

> **Purpose: To learn cooking skills, measuring.**
> **Materials Needed: Ingredients below.**

Parent/ Teacher: Cooking teaches many skills, including measuring.

Directions:

(1) Ingredients:
  1 C. light corn syrup
  1/2 C. sugar
  1 pkg. gelatin, flavored
  1/2 pound peanuts
  9 C. popped corn
(2) Bring the sugar and syrup to a boil
(3) Remove from the stove and add gelatin. Sir.
(4) Add peanuts. Pour mixture over popcorn.
(5) When cool enough to touch, form into balls.

-209-

DECISION-MAKING

> **Purpose: To learn how to make decisions.**
> **Materials Needed: None.**

Parent/ Teacher: If you are always making every decision for your child, then she will not learn how to make decisions for herself. An activity such as this helps her develop her own decision-making skills. There is a delicate balance between allowing a child some decision-making ability and letting the child become controlling.

Directions:

(1) When it's time for your child to dress in the morning, ask her what she wants to wear. Let her pick out her own clothes.
(2) When deciding on a meal, allow her some choices, such as "Would you care for macaroni and cheese or spaghetti?" In restaurants, give her choices from the menu.
(3) When picking an activity, ask her, "Would you care to go to the park or to the library?"

-210-

WOOD PROJECTS

Purpose: To learn shape concepts, simple construction, motor skills.
Materials Needed: Wood scraps, sandpaper, glue.

Parent/ Teacher: This is a great activity for kids to do with their dads. A shop teacher told me about it because while he was in the garage developing projects for his students, his kids could be entertained and educated with wood scraps.

Directions:

(1) Give your child several wood scraps, sandpaper, and glue.
(2) Tell her to build something with the materials. Show her how to use sandpaper.

-211-

LEARNING TO BALANCE

> **Purpose: To develop balance. This is a learned skill that is important for future learning.**
> **Materials Needed: Chalk, straight board.**

Parent/ Teacher: Do the following activities with your child until he can walk a straight line. Don't forget to praise your child for trying, even if he is not able to master the skill right away, by saying, "I'm glad you're trying," or "You're getting better."

Directions:

(1) Draw a straight line on the sidewalk with chalk.
(2) Walk on the line to show your child how it's done.
(3) Have your child walk a narrow path.
(4) Now have your child stand on one foot until you count to 10.
(5) Show your child how to walk on a raised board or a curb.
(6) Show your child how to walk with heel touching toe and arms spread out for balance.

-212-

CLEANING THE PARK

Purpose: To learn to be part of the community, social skills.
Materials Needed: Trash bags.

Parent/ Teacher: Praise your child for helping keep the park clean.

Directions:

(1) Go to a park. Explain to your child that keeping our areas clean of litter is important for health, safety, and the environment.
(2) Give her a trash a bag and tell her to pick up trash.

KEEP OUR COMMUNITY CLEAN

-213-

THE BIRTHDAY CAKE

> **Purpose: To learn to follow directions.**
> **Materials Needed: Paper, crayons.**

Parent/ Teacher: Give your child paper and crayons, and give her the instructions below.

Instructions:

(1) Draw a pink birthday cake.
(2) Put six blue candles on it.
(3) Draw two purple birthday gifts beside it.
(4) Draw two people at the party.
(5) Draw five balloons with strings.

-214-

HUMPTY DUMPTY & LITTLE MISS MUFFET

> **Purpose: To develop language recognition.**
> **Materials Needed: Paper, crayons.**

Parent/ Teacher: Teach your child these nursery rhymes and then have the child draw Humpty Dumpty on a wall or Little Miss Muffet.

Rhymes:

Humpty Dumpty

Humpty Dumpty sat on a wall.
Humpty Dumpty had a great fall.
All the king's horses
And all the king's men
Couldn't put Humpty Dumpty
Back together again.

Little Miss Muffet

Little Miss Muffet
Sat on a tuffet
Eating her curds and whey.
Along came a spider
And sat down beside her
And frightened Miss Muffet away.

-215-

DOCTOR'S BAG

**Purpose: To learn about basic first aid, science.
Materials Needed: Medicine cabinet or first aid
   kit.**

Parent/ Teacher: Explore medicine cabinet with your child. Besides explaining what things are for, you can also teach them caution in what not to get into.

Directions:

(1) Take a group of items from the medicine cabinet and put them in an old purse. Explain to your child that this is her "doctor's bag".

(2) Some of the items in the bag can be:

Band Aids	Vaseline	Cotton balls
Cotton Swabs	Gauze	Lotions
Thermometer		

(3) Let your child use the doctor's bag and play doctor to her dolls. She can play veterinarian to her pet too, as long as you supervise.

(4) This is a good chance to explain to your child that doctors and nurses are helpers, that we keep our bodies healthy by exercise and good nutrition, and that we don't take medicine that's not ours.

-216-

BEING THANKFUL

Purpose: To learn good social skills.
Materials Needed: None.

Parent/ Teacher: Your child should know that Thanksgiving is not the only time we should be thankful.

Directions:

(1) Tell your child what it means to be thankful.
(2) Explain that sometimes we should tell people we are thankful for the nice things that they have done.
(3) Let your child dictate a note to someone for something for which they are thankful.
(4) Have your child draw a picture of the things for which she is thankful.

I will find the good things around me.

I will be thankful today.

-217-

ENDING SOUNDS

> **Purpose: Language arts.**
> **Materials Needed: Pencil.**

Parent/ Teacher: Have your child match the letter to the word that ends in that sound. Use the words sun and storm.

Directions:

(1) Tell your child, "It had been raining. Then the sun came out and then—" Let your child draw what happens.
(2) Tell your child, "Flowers were growing nicely. Then hail came and—" Let your child draw what happens.

n

m

-218-

STORMY DAY

> **Purpose: To develop general knowledge and thinking and listening skills, to encourage creative movement.**
> **Materials Needed: None.**

Parent/ Teacher: This is a stormy day activity. Two books to enjoy and read in addition to the activities are: *The Snowy Day* by Ezra Jack Keats (Viking, 1962) easily found in the library, about a little boy's fun in the snow; *Rain* by Peter Spier (Doubleday, 1982) a wordless book that tells how to enjoy the rain.

Directions:

(1) Start by saying, "As the storm goes by, we see the lightning, then we hear the thunder, and then the wind. We see dark, dark clouds, and hear big raindrops falling on the roof and the sidewalk and the grass and in the trees. When it is all finished, the sun will come out again to dry up the rain, and sometimes we can see a rainbow. Let's see if we can pretend that we are the dark clouds, or the rain, or the sun."
(2) Try having the child make the following using creative movement. With several children, this can be a drama activity.
Dark Clouds: Have the child curve his arms and hands overhead and show strong facial expressions.
Big Raindrops: Have the child fill his cheeks full of air, and curve his arms to show a fat, round raindrop.
Lightning: Have the child make slashing motions with arms.
Wind: Have the child make howling noises and blow.
Thunder: Have the child make crashing noises.

-219-

GIVING REASONS

> **Purpose: To learn reasoning skills, vocabulary.**
> **Materials Needed: None.**

Parent/ Teacher: Children develop reasoning skills by being allowed to figure things out.

Directions:

(1) Prepare an activity that has several steps, such as changing the battery in a clock. The steps are:
   a. Remove the old battery.
   b. Decide what kind of battery is needed.
   c. Replace the battery.
(2) Ask the child if she knows what the first step is to the activity. Then ask, "What is the reason that you believe that is the first step?"
(3) Do the first step. Ask the child again what the next step is. Again, ask, "What is the reason that you believethat is the next step?"
(4) Repeat asking reasons from the child throughout the activity.

-220-

WHAT'S MISSING?

> **Purpose: To develop visual memory.**
> **Materials Needed: Small objects.**

Parent/ Teacher: This activity will help your child develop visual memory.

Directions:

(1) Take several common household objects and put them in a pile. Five objects is a good number to start with. Suggestions: pen, paper clip, spoon, thimble, scissors.
(2) Tell your child to look at the pile and see what's there.
(3) Have your child close his eyes while you mix up the objects and remove one of them.
(4) Ask your child to tell your which object is missing.
(5) Try this several times. When your child has mastered doing it with five objects, you can increase the number of objects you use.

-221-

JUMP OVER THE CREEK

Purpose: To develop motor coordination.
Materials Needed: None.

Parent/ Teacher: Jumping skills are important to learn at this age.
Practice other jumping activities, such as jump rope.

Directions:

(1) Make a pretend creek using blankets.
(2) Have your child jump from one side of the creek to the other.
(3) Make the creek wider and wider.

-222-

TELL ME ABOUT—

Purpose: Language arts.
Materials Needed: Pictures from magazines.

Parent/ Teacher: Find pictures of actions or sequence that can be predicted.

Directions:

(1) Look at a picture with your child.
(2) Say, "Tell me about this picture."
(3) Let the child give his description of the picture.
(4) You can ask for more information by saying, "And then what would happen?"
(5) You can keep on asking "Tell me about—" for pictures or about items in the room, or about activities the child likes.

-223-

RECEIVING MAIL

> **Purpose: To encourage an interest in reading.**
> **Materials Needed: Subcription to magazines or**
> **book clubs.**

Parent/ Teacher: Your child will enjoy receving mail. To ensure that he receives mail on a regular basis, subscribe to a magazine or a book club. One highly recommended magazine is *Highlights for Children.*

-224-

RUNNING THROUGH SPRINKLERS

> **Purpose: Physical education, fun.**
> **Materials Needed: Sprinkler.**

Parent/ Teacher: This activity provides a lot of enjoyment for the children on a hot day. There's learning skills happening, but hey—who cares?

Directions:

(1) Run through the sprinklers with your children. You'll be amazed at the amount of physical exertion they are using just by running, jumping, and screaming.

(2) Point out the rainbow that's created by the water.

(3) Jump over the sprinkler.

(4) Take a plastic ball and hold it over the stream and let it go flying.

(5) Hold the sprinkler to stop the water flow, then let it go.

(6) Outrun the sprinkler.

-225-

ALIKE OR NOT ALIKE

Purpose: To learn similarities and differences.
Materials Needed: None.

Parent/ Teacher: Knowing about similarities and differences is important, as this will help the child recognize the differences in letters and words when learning to read.

Directions:

(1) Using familiar household objects, ask your child, "How is the table like the chair?" (Both are made of wood. Both have four legs.)
(2) Then ask, "How are they different?" (One is for sitting at, one is for sitting beside. One is square, one is round.)
(3) Ask the same questions about other objects.
(4) Then ask the child, "How many objects in the room are made of plastic?" "How many objects in the room are made of wood?"

-226-

BUNCHES

Parent/ Teacher: Your child can learn to count by 2's and 3's up to at least 20.

Directions:

(1) Using rubber bands, have your child make bundles of common objects. For instance, makes bundles of 2. She should find two pencils, wrap them with a rubber band. Then find two spoons, wrap them with a rubber band.
(2) Then count by 2's using the bundles.
(2) Repeat the activity using a different number, such as 3. Then count by 3's.

-227-

PHOTO ALBUMS, VIDEO TAPES

Purpose: To about self and family.
Materials Needed: Family photos or videos.

Parent/ Teacher: Your child learns at lot about himself, his parents, his grandparents and extended family from photo albums and video tapes.

Directions:

(1) Show your child your wedding pictures and tell her about your wedding.

(2) Show her your childhood pictures with pictures of her grandparents and aunts and uncles when they were younger. Talk about the things you liked to do when you were a child. Tell her family stories: jokes they played on each other; how Aunt Doris was always late to school and blamed "The Leprechaun"; how Grandpa liked to eat raw unions.

(3) Show her pictures of herself when she was a baby. Say things like, "Then you couldn't even feed yourself, and now you are old enough to cook!" Children like to see their baby pictures to know that they really belong. If adopted, you should show them pictures of the day they were adopted and tell how happy everyone was.

(4) Point out things that help them see who they are and who the family is. You can use this time to build family connections and stress the importance of family relationships. You can stress values, like loyalty. "Grandpa went off to the war and Grandma waited for him because she loved him. They have been married over 50 years."

-228-

LEARNING TO SKIP

> **Purpose: To develop large muscle control and skipping ability.**
> **Materials Needed: None.**

Parent/ Teacher: If your child has not yet learned to skip, pick a sunny day to teach her. She will love skipping. Sing the following song.

Song:

Skip to My Lou

Skip, skip, skip to my lou,
Skip, skip, skip to my lou,
Skip, skip, skip to my lou,
Skip to my lou, my darling.

Hop, hop, hop to my lou.
Hop, hop, hop to my lou,
Hop, hop, hop to my lou,
Hop to my lou, my darling.

-229-

RESPONSIBILITY

> **Purpose: To learn about responsibility, values.**
> **Materials Needed: None.**

Parent/ Teacher: A child learns responsibility most effectively by being given chores and being expected to do them consistently.

Directions:

(1) Give your child a regular chore: taking out recycling materials; picking up his toys; taking care of a pet. This chore is his responsibility as his contribution to the family, and not to be paid for. If you want to teach him about earning money, see the next activity.

(2) Teach him that responsibility also means to accept the results of our actions without blaming someone else. If he fails to do his work, or does it poorly, excuses will not be acceptable.

(3) Role-play about accepting responsibility for our actions. Say, "What would you say if you spilled milk at the table?" "What would you do if you broke your sister's necklace?"

I am responsible for my own work.
I am responsible for my own actions.

-230-

EARNING MONEY

Purpose: To learn how to earn money.
Materials Needed: None.

Parent/ Teacher: This idea was given to me by a friend who used it with his son, who turned out to be a very responsible adult.

Directions:

(1) Your child needs to be responsible for a certain amount of chores without being paid. However, additional chores can have a dollar amount attached. These optional chores can be done only after the regular chores have all been finished for the week. Then the child can select from the list of the paid chores. This helps teach the child that certain things must be done because we are a member of the family, but that there are ways to earn money above our required chores. (2) Make a list of these regular and optional chores and post in a conspicuous place.

REGULAR CHORES	PAID CHORES (all regular chores must be finished first)
take out newspapers	wash car $5
feed pet	bathe pet $2
pick up toys	help carry in groceries $2
wash dinner dishes on Tuesday, Thursday	wash dishes extra day $1

-231-

HOW MANY WAYS?

> **Purpose: Language arts, general knowledge.**
> **Materials Needed: None.**

Parent/ Teacher: These questions also encourage creativity.

Directions:

(1) Ask your child, "How many ways can we use a glass?"
(2) Ask, "How many ways can we use a chair?"
(3) "How many ways can we use paper?"
(4) Let your child ask, "How many ways—?" to you.

-232-

"FREEZE!"

> **Purpose: To develop muscle control.**
> **Materials Needed: None.**

Parent/ Teacher: This activity will help your child learn how to control his movement.

Directions:

(1) Have your child walk around the room normally. Say, "Freeze!" and he must stop all movement, just as if he were frozen.
(2) He has to stay in that position until you say, "Melt!"
(3) Then he can walk around again. Have him do exaggerated movements, like swinging his arms or marching like a soldier.
(4) Again, say, "Freeze!" and he must stay in that position until you say, "Melt!"

-233-

BECOME AN ORANGE PEEL OR A DRUM

> **Purpose: To learn creative movement.**
> **Materials Needed: None.**

Parent/ Teacher: Ask your child to create the following objects with their body movements.

Objects:

(1) An orange being peeled.
(2) A tulip coming out of the ground in the spring.
(3) A computer screen.
(4) Water from a faucet.
(5) A balloon with air coming out of it.
(6) Boiling water.
(7) A puppy learning to walk.
(8) Weeds blowing in the wind.
(9) Paper being folded.
(10) A pen writing on paper.
(11) A drum being played.

-234-

SORTING LEAVES

Purpose: To learn how to sort and classify.
Materials Needed: Leaves, book on leaves.

Parent/ Teacher: Autumn is the best time to do this.

Directions:

(1) Collect about five leaves from different kinds of trees.
(2) Spread them on the table and look at the differences.
(3) Using a leaf book, find the name of the kind of leaf each one is.
(4) The child can make her own poster by gluing the leaves on poster board and she can write the name of the leaf with a marker below each leaf.

-235-

CARD DECK ACTIVITIES

Purpose: Math skills.
Materials Needed: Card deck.

Parent/ Teacher: Numerous math skills can be learned with a simple card deck.

Directions:

(1) Have your child count the number of red cards.
(2) Have your child count the number of face cards.
(3) Give her 5 cards and have her put them in order.
(4) Find the differences in the face cards.
(5) Play "In Between" by laying two cards down. Ask your child if the next card will be in between those cards.
(6) Play a memory game with cards.
(7) Start simple addition with cards. Ask your child to add the scores from cards.

-236-

FOLLOWING THE RULES

**Purpose: To be able to anticipate outcomes and
consequences of actions.**
Materials Needed: None.

Parent/ Teacher: Have a discussion about the importance of rules.
Explain the purpose of rules, which is to protect your child. Discuss
what can happen if rules are broken. Make a clear connection between
the breaking of a rule and the result of doing so.

Directions:

(1) Play a game with your child and deliberately break a rule.
Ask your child what happened. Ask your child how breaking the rule changes the game.

(2) Discuss what happens when adults break the rules and
drive too fast. Explain that adult can pay the consequences
by getting a speeding ticket or by having an accident.

(3) As you and your child go places, continue to discover the
rules, discussing the reasons for such rules and what happens as a result of breaking those rules. For example, a rule
at the zoo says, "Do not feed the animals." It's there to
protect the health of the animals. Breaking that rule could get
you thrown out of the zoo or could harm the animals.

I can follow the rules.

-237-

VISIT A POLICE STATION

Purpose: To develop respect, responsibility, general knowledge, and expressive oral language.
Materials Needed: Transporation to a local police station.

Parent/ Teacher: Call your local police station and make arrangements for you and your child to visit. Encourage your child to ask questions.

Directions:

(1) After the visit, discuss again why we have police—to protect us and help us in time of emergency. Make sure you convey a respectful attitude towards police.
(2) Encourage your child to talk about the visit to the police station while you write exactly what she says. Compliment your child for using good manners and good behavior at the police station.
(3) Write in the journal about your trip.

-238-

TWENTY QUESTIONS

> **Purpose: Observation, problem-solving.**
> **Materials Needed: None.**

Parent/ Teacher: This timeless game is very useful for working with kids. It's also a great way to keep the kids occupied on a long trip. Your child can be quite tireless in asking questions, so might as well put it to good use.

Directions:

(1) Pick an object in the room and say, "I'm thinking of something."
(2) The child is allowed to ask questions that can be answered yes or no. "Is it on the wall?" "Is it black?" "Does it have pictures on it?"
(3) His questions and your answers will lead him to discover what the object is.

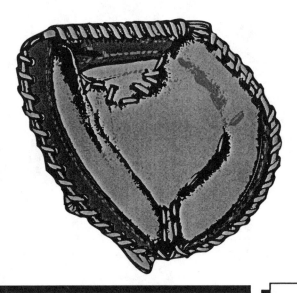

-239-

TREE RINGS

Purpose: Science knowledge.
Materials Needed: A tree stump.

Parent/ Teacher: This activity can be extra special if you live near an old-growth forest and can do this activity there.

Directions:

(1) Discuss what happens to a tree as it gets older.
(2) Find a tree stump.
(3) Explain to the child that each year in the life of a tree, it adds another ring. This ring represents the growth for that year.
(4) Point out that there are wide rings and narrow rings. Ask the child if he can figure out why the rings are different sizes. (Depends on the availability of rain and sunlight that year.)
(5) Count the rings together to figure out the age of the tree.

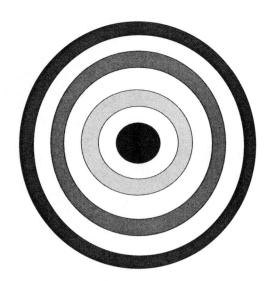

-240-

HAND TRACING

> **Purpose:** To develop body awareness, small muscle coordination, hand-to-eye coordination.
>
> **Materials Needed:** Pencil or crayon, paper.

Parent/ Teacher: Children enjoy tracing their hands and other body parts. You might want to do this activity with their bare feet as well.

Directions:

(1) Have your child look at his hand. Now have the child look at the hand on this page. Are they alike or different?
(2) Have your child place his hand on paper. Let him trace his own hand with a pencil or a crayon.

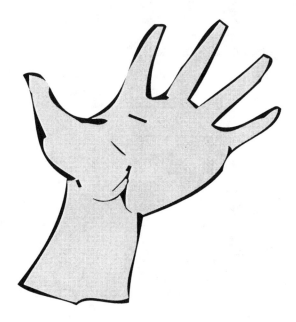

-241-

SORTING CLOTHES

> **Purpose:** To develop the ability to classify according to categories; also helps develop responsible habits.
>
> **Materials Needed:** Laundry pile.

Parent/ Teacher: Before doing the family laundry, ask your child to put all the socks in one pile, the shirts in one pile, towels in one pile, etc. After you help your child do this, she will enjoy sorting the clothes by color.

-242-

ROCK ART

> **Purpose:** Art, creativity.
> **Materials Needed:** Rocks, paints, brushes.

Parent/ Teacher: Gather several smooth stones for this activity.

Directions:

(1) Wash and dry the stones.
(2) Let the children paint faces on the stones. You can add yarn for hair or use seeds for eyes.
(3) The children may also want to paint other things on the stones, such as flowers, trees, animals, etc.

-243-

OIL & WATER

Purpose: Basic science.
Materials Needed: Jar, oil, and water.

Parent/ Teacher: This can be as entertaining to your child as a lava lamp, and much less expensive!

Directions:

(1) Fill a jar half full with water, and add vegetable oil to the other half.
(2) Add a few drops of food coloring.
(3) Put on lid and shake.
(4) Your child can watch the oil and water wiggle and move and make designs. Explain that oil and water are different and do not mix.

-244-

FINISHING

> **Purpose: To learn it's important to finish.**
> **Materials Needed: Poster board, markers.**

Parent/ Teacher: Finishing a project once it's started should be explained to a child.

Directions:

(1) Talk about why we do things and why it's important to finish. Talk about "doers" versus "wanna-doers".
(2) Discuss things that are important to finish: chores, school, promises.
(3) Talk about taking breaks to make a chore seem less burdensome. Explain how a big job can be broken down into smaller pieces so that it's easier to accomplish.
(4) Make a poster like the one below and let the child draw on it.

I can finish the things I start.

-245-

DRAWING CONCLUSIONS

> **Purpose:** Sequence skills.
> **Materials Needed:** Paper, crayons.

Parent/ Teacher: Have your child draw the conclusion to each of the clues below.

Directions:

(1) Jackie opened her presents. There was a dog bone, a dog collar, and a dog dish. Her mother said that there was another present in the next room. What is that present?
(2) Simon smelled good sweeet smells coming from the oven. He saw pots and pans in the sink. He saw his mother taking a cooky sheet from the oven. What did he smell?
(3) Moesha heard a clicking noise as she came home. She saw water on the sidewalk. What was in the yard?
(4) Marty heard thunder in the distance. Then he saw lightning and felt the wind. He felt a drop of rain on his cheek. He reached for something and opened it. What did he open?

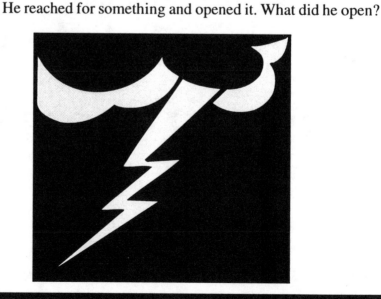

-246-

BACKWARDS

> **Purpose: Physical education, coordination.**
> **Materials Needed: Blanket.**

Parent/ Teacher: With several children, you can have contests doing the following activities.

Directions:

(1) Ask the child to walk and run backwards. Show him the area you want him to do this in.
(2) Have him jump backwards over a blanket.
(3) Show him how to do the crab walk, and then ask him to do the crab walk backwards.
(4) Have him hop like a bunny, only backwards.
(5) Ask him what else he can do backwards.

-247-

ORGANIZING

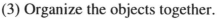

Purpose: To develop organizing skills.
Materials Needed: Household materials.

Parent/ Teacher: This can be done with a variety of materials. The main idea is to let your child learn how to organize.

Directions:

(1) Gather a group of household objects that need organizing. Ideas include:
    a. Office objects: staples, paper clips, scissors, pens.
    b. Kitchen objects: silverware, utencils.
    c. Workshop objects: nails, glue, small tools.
(2) Tell the child that you would like to organize the objects in a fashion that's convenient to use. Let the child make recommendations.
(3) Organize the objects together.

-248-

PLANT ART

**Purpose: To develop small muscle control, visual
discrimination, and creativity.**
**Materials Needed: Scraps of fabric with floral
patterns, felt markers, white paper, glue,
poster board, scissors.**

Parent/ Teacher: Discuss "inches" and "colors" as you and your child
gather materials.

Directions:

(1) Cut out the flowers, leaves, stems and buds from the
floral fabric. You may cut a pattern and then let the child try
cutting also.
(2) Use the colored marker to outline the shapes on the white
paper.
(3) Glue the shapes on the poster board.
(4) Cut the floral shapes.
(5) Now you have flowers that can be arranged anyway your
child wants.

-249-

THINKING QUESTIONS

Purpose: Thinking, reasoning.
Materials Needed: None.

Parent/ Teacher: Ask your child the following questions. Let her ponder the answers and help lead her with more questions, if necessary.

Questions:

(1) What color is the sunset?
(2) Can eagles walk?
(3) Is orange a color or a fruit?
(3) Is lemon a color?
(4) Do bees <u>hum</u> or <u>sting</u>?
(5) When we say that a turkey gobbles, do we mean that it eats or that it makes a noise?
(6) Does the moon shine in the daytime?
(7) Where does the sun go at night?
(8) Does a bed have <u>sheets</u> or <u>shirts</u>?
(9) Is ice frozen or boiling?
(10) Do we have <u>sheets</u> of paper or <u>shirts</u> of paper?

-250-

CREATIVE SQUARES

> **Purpose:** Creativity, visual association.
> **Materials Needed:** Crayons, colored pencils.

Parent/ Teacher: Have your child make pictures from the squares with circles below. Each square should be a different picture.

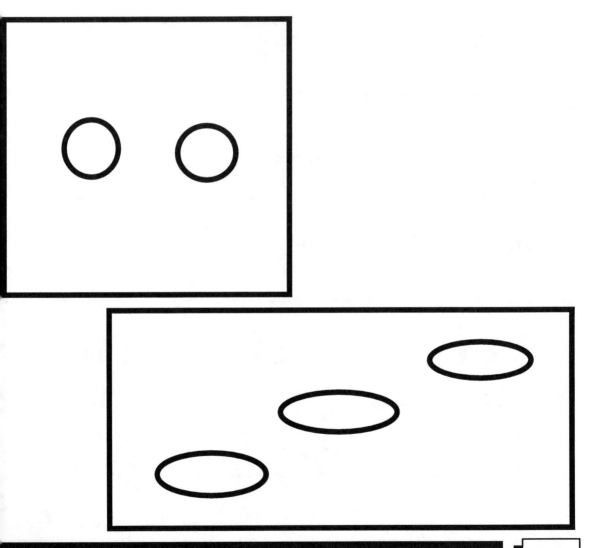

-251-

SAME WORDS

Purpose: Language arts.
Materials Needed: Pencil

Parent/ Teacher: Have your child circle the words that are the same.

be	bug	be
in	in	at
go	am	go
cat	rat	rat
man	man	pin

-252-

POSITIVE ATTITUDE

Purpose: Social skills.
Materials Needed: Poster board, markers.

Parent/ Teacher: Positive attitudes are catchy. Let your child catch yours!

Directions:

(1) Tell your child what it means to have a positive attitude.
(2) Explain what it means to expect that good things will happen.
(3) Talk about expressions, such as "Find the silver lining behind every cloud," or "Expect the best and get it." Think of other positive expressions.
(4) Help your child make a poster like the one below and let him decorate it.

Today I will expect good things to happen.

-253-

DODGE BALL

Purpose: Physical education, motor skills.
Materials Needed: Soft rubber ball.

Parent/ Teacher: This works well with a group of children.

Directions:

(1) In the yard or in the park, find a way to divide the area in half.
(2) Divide into two teams.
(3) One team throws the ball at the players on the other team. The team being thrown at should dodge the ball.
(4) With several players, a person who is hit by the ball sits out until a new game begins. If you are playing alone with your child, you can alter the game by adding scoring for each time a player hits the other player with the ball.

-254-

OPPOSITES

Parent/ Teacher: Read the following words to your child, and ask her to match the opposites by drawing a line between the two words.

happy	**whisper**
laugh	**sad**
shout	**cry**
asleep	**hate**
love	**awake**

-255-

HOW THE SUN MOVES

> **Purpose: Simple science, vocabulary.**
> **Materials Needed: Flashlight, rubber ball.**

Parent/ Teacher: Your child will be fascinated about how the earth spins and rotates around the sun.

Directions:

(1) Using a flashlight and a rubber ball, show how the earth turns each day, causing day and night.
(2) You can also show how the earth tilts, causing seasons to the northern and southern hemispheres.
(3) Show the child how the earth moves around the sun during the year.

-256-

APPLE DOLLS

> **Purpose: Art, creativity.**
> **Materials Needed: Apples, fabric, decorations.**

Parent/ Teacher: Dry out several apples ahead of time for this activity.

Directions:

(1) Ask your child to look at a dried apple and see if there's a face that you can see.
(2) Using the face that you already see, add decorations to make the apple into a doll.
(3) You can use yarn for hair, colored sewing pins for eyes or nose, fabric for a dress.
(4) Your child can get as creative as she wishes with this activity. These make great gifts!

-257-

WINNERS READ

Purpose: Encouraging reading.
Materials Needed: Poster board, markers.

Parent/ Teacher: Encourage your child to read. Let her know that readers are winners, and winners read! Make a poster like the one below and decorate together. Place in a conspicuous place.

Readers are winners and winners read!

BIBLIOGRAPHY

This bibliography has been adapted from *Success Starts Early* by Stan Wonderley, also form Blue Bird Publishing. There are books appropriate for 3 to 7 year olds, but they are all included here because each child develops his own unique rate.

BOOKS FOR THREE- AND FOUR-YEAR-OLDS

Three- and four-year-olds are emerging from the frustration of their own inabilities. They are still struggling to gain mastery over their physical skills and developing competence in verbal communications. They are able to use language to express most of their needs, emotions, and ideas. They are ale to run, jump, spin, and climb more freely.

Children this age will enjoy picture books about independence, imaginary friends, scary stories--real and unreal--fairytales, folktales, and fantasy. They enjoy stories with simple plots. They want to know about themselves when they were babies, as well as about relatives and extended family. This is a time to read stories about friends, such as *Best Friends* by Miriam Cohen. They'll enjoy the plot in wordless books. The illustrations carry the plot. While the family is have "read-at-home time," your three- to four-year-old will enjoy "reading" wordless books.

Books for this age and numerous and fun to read aloud. If read to two or three times daily, they will probably learn to read on their own. Now that's exciting parent and child.

Here are ten books every three- and four-year-olds should know:

The Carrot Seed by Ruth Krauss. Harper and Row, 1945. This classic about the determined little planter will be read many times.
Curious George by H. A. Rey. Houghton Mifflin, 1941. This classic has delighted children with his scary situations, from which he is always rescued by "the man in the yellow hat."
Freight Train by Donald Crews. Green Willow, 1984. It's always fun to watch freight trains go by. You'll want to count the cars.
Gilberto and the Wind by Marie Hall. Viking, 1963. Don't let your child not experience this book about a boy and the wind--how it sounds, what it blows, what it breaks, and what a little boy can do with it.
The Little Red Hen. Clarion Books, 1973. The irresistible pictures and an old tale are just right to please threes and fours.
Make Way for Ducklings by Robert McCoskey. Viking, 1941. Children of all ages will enjoy the ducklings and their mother crossing the street with the help of a policeman.

May I Bring a Friend? by Beatrice Schenk de Regniers. Atheneum, 1964. This wonderful read-aloud book will delight children from three and up, as the animals are welcomed to tea by the king and queen.

Poems to Read to the Very Young, selected by Josette Frank. Random House, 1982. These well-selected poems have been a favorite for a long time.

The Snowy Day by Ezra Jack Keats. Viking, 1962. The simple words and glowing pictures tell of a little boy's fun in the snow.

The Tale of Peter Rabbit by Beatrix Potter. Warne, 1902. This classic is about savoring power and independence. For all children who love a little suspense and danger.

BOOKS FOR FIVE-YEAR-OLDS

When selecting books for your five-year-old, the text can be longer and language less simple. Their attention spans of fives are growing like the rest of them. So they can sit still longer and deal with a more complex story.

Your goal should be developing a love of books and reading. When your child grows up with a rich diet of wonderful books, the appetite for learning to read falls into place. Naturally, rather than having to be hammered in by others, learning to read should be easy. It will be if you read to your five-year-old as often as she wants to be read to.

Your five-year-old will enjoy fantasy (such as Ramona the Pest or Fredrick's Fables), books about animals, big things that go (such as Little Toot), and stories without books (your tales of when your were little).

They begin to get the idea that we read a book from left to right. They'll tell about the picture. All you need to do is read the text, then let him/her tell about the picture.

Many five-year-olds will be reading before they start to school in the first grade. By reading and discussing stories, learning to read should be an easy task--as easy as learning to talk and walk. It almost becomes a natural thing to do. You will also want your child seeing you reading and enjoying a book.

Here are nine books every five-year-old should know:

Bedtime for Francis by Russel Hoban. Harper and Row, 1960. This book has become a classic. Francis the badger is in bed singing the alphabet, until she gets to "T." Kids will identify with the little badger's problem.

Caps for Sale by Esphyr Slobodkina. Addison-Wesley, 1947. This classic will be loved by children, especially the repetition and power of telling those monkey-see-monkey-do thieves to "give me back my cap!"

The Little Engine That Could by Watty Piper. Buccaneer Books, 1981. This classic tale of determination and belief in oneself first came out in the thirties.

Mike Mulligan and His Steam Shovel by Virginia Lee Barton. Houghton Mifflin, 1939. A meaningful tale about faithful friends and about "new" not necessarily being best.

Millions of Cats by Wanda Gag. Coward, McCann, 1928. This classic folktale is the story of a very old man who set out to look for one sweet fluffy feline and returned with "hundreds of cats."

Nutshell Library by Maurice Sendak. Harper and Row, 1962. This book contains four gems: Chicken Soup and Rice, One Was Johnny, Pierre, and Alligators All Around. You'll find a counting book, alphabet book, a moral tale, and a romp through the seasons.

The Runaway Bunny by Margaret Wise Brown. Harper and Row, 1942. A tender-loving tale of a little bunny who dreams of runaway adventure and a loving mom who reassures her runaway that she'll never be far away.

Stone Soup by Marcia Brown. Scribners, 1947. This classic tale about three hungry soldiers and how they made soup with three stones plus a dash of cunning and humor. You could make stone soup for dinner. The ingredients are in the book.

The Story About Ping by Marjorie Flack. Penguin, 1977. Five-year-olds can easily relate to this tale about a duck that does not want to get spanked for being the last one home.

BOOKS FOR SIX- AND SEVEN-YEAR-OLDS

Books for sixes and sevens take on a new dimension. These are the years when children get started with the formal business of learning to read. It is also the time when most parents stop reading to their kids. This is a time when you'll want to listen to your child read and then continue to read stories a year or so above their reading ability. Their listening comprehension is at least two years above their reading ability. Easy-to-read books begin to loose their appeal at a time when they have a rich need for listening to good children's literature.

Their ability to understand complex plots goes well beyond their word-attack skills. You can provide them with easy-to-read books, but they also need challenging books to grow into. They will enjoy "rereading" the books you read during the fives. They may read them over and over.

Reading for six- and seven-year-olds is a bridge to understanding that other people have problems, feelings, and experiences like their own. A good story invites the children to step outside themselves into someone else's shoes for awhile. Kids at this age experience a wide range of feelings, and they can begin to understand them through good literature.

They enjoy books about independence and interdependence, such as *Where the Wild Things Are*. Max is on his own, he faces the unknown. Kids enjoy books about family and independence in the family, such as *Alexander and the Terrible, Horrible, No Good, Very Bad Day,* in which Alexander begins to understand that everyone has days in which nothing goes right.

They can handle books about dealing with siblings, as in Worse Than Willy, in which two siblings complain to their grandpa about their new baby brother.

They relish humor and usually have a firm fix on fantasy and reality. They enjoy two green monsters tiptoeing into a bedroom, as in *Pleasant Dreams*. They love to hear folktales, both old and new. My grandkids always enjoyed my telling them stores about life when I was a boy their age. They love fairytales of all sorts--stories like those in *The Big Golden Book of Fairytales*. Then there are those wonderful wordless book, like *The Mystery of the Giant Foot Print*.

They want to read and hear books about real things, too, like in *Dinosaur Time*. Then there are the concept books, such as *Trucks You Can Count On*.

This is not a time to quit reading aloud to your children. These read-aloud sessions might include a younger sibling or an older one. I read *Charlotte's Web* to my second-grade grandson, and his fifth-grade brother listened in and enjoyed it. I can recall listening to *Gone With the Wind* being read to my 12- and 14-year-old brothers. It was always a happy time to hear my mother's reading voice.

Here are ten books every six- and seven-year-old should know:

Alexander and the Terrible, Horrible, No Good, Very Bad Day by Judith Viorst. Atheneum, 1972. Everyone has days when nothing goes right, when you wish you had stayed in bed--or left for Australia. Alexander's complaints are both recognizable and laughable.
Amos and Boris by William Steig. Penguin, 1977. This is a perfect math for six- and seven-year-olds about Amos the mouse and Boris the whale, who are the closest of friends.
The Fairy Tale Treasure by Virginia Haviland. Conrad, McCann, 1972. One of the best collections of old favorites for this age group.
Frog and Toad Are Friends by Arnold Lobel. Harper and Row, 1970. In an easy-to-read format, these short stories about two loyal friends can be enjoyed as read-aloud. They're right on target in feelings. Also, Frog and Toad Together, Frog and Toad All Year, and Days with Frog and Toad.
Go, Dog, Go by P. D. Eastman. Random House, 1961. Action-packed dogs with plenty of zany humor to add story to limited text.
The House at Pooh Corner by A. A. Milne. Dutton, 1961. This is a great read-aloud story with rich language. Great pen and ink illustrations, too.
Ramona the Pest by Beverly Cleary. Morrow, 1968. Ramona is in kindergarten and is having trouble with the teacher and a classmate on how things are "'sposed" to be. Also, Ramona the Brave and others.
The Snowman by Raymond Briggs. Random House, 1978. This exquisite fantasy about a boy and his snowman who take off on a thrilling adventure is the stuff snowflakes and daydreams are made of.
Steve by John Steptoe. Harper and Row, 1969. This is a touching story of Little Steve who lives with another family. Robert, an only child, is bother with Steve and "his old spoiled self."

Where the Wild Things Are by Maurice Sendak. Harper and Row, 1963. When Max, who's been acting like a "wild thing," is sent to bed without supper, he takes off on an adventure that leads to a special place where he becomes king.

The Cricket in Times Square by George Selden. Straus and Giroux, 1960. It all begins when Chester, a cricket from Connecticut, gets whisked off in a picnic basket and finds himself in Times Square Subway Station. This is a story of friendship, cooperation and a taste of fame. A treat for the whole family.

Dominic by William Steig. Straus and Giroux, 1972. This is a wonderful story about courage and imagination along life's highway. The ever-present danger of the Doomsday Robbers awaits, but Dominic, the young hero, is around with a magic spear that helps him carve out his own identity.

A PARENTING TITLE
FROM BLUE BIRD PUBLISHING

ISBN 0-933025-51-3
$14.95

DISCOVER THE SECRET INGREDIENT
TO SUCCESSFUL PARENTING!

This insightful and useful guide to bringing together all the elements of good parenting includes 20 general guidelines for good parenting, 25 guidelines for establishing a good relationship with your child, and 15 keys to communication with your child.

"Its carefully labeled segments, insightful questions, and 'Possible Pitfalls' makes this a reader and parent-friendly book, one which helps us love both ourselves and our children in a more nourishing way."—Sue Patton Thoele, author of *Heart-Centered Marriage*.

Available at bookstores and libraries.

ANOTHER EDUCATIONAL TITLE FROM BLUE BIRD PUBLISHING

ISBN 0-933025-17-3
$15.95

PHONICS!!

This program has been adopted by many Literacy Groups and Right-to-Read groups across the United States and Canada.

Available at bookstores and libraries.

ANOTHER EDUCATIONAL TITLE FROM BLUE BIRD PUBLISHING

ISBN 0-933025-47-5
$12.95 4th edition

A HOMESCHOOLING BESTSELLER!

This homeschool classic has been reviewed by
*Booklist, Library Journal, Home Education Magazine,
New Big Book of Home Learning*, and many more.

Available at bookstores and libraries.

ANOTHER EDUCATIONAL TITLE FROM BLUE BIRD PUBLISHING

ISBN 0-933025-48-3
$12.95 4th edition

A HOMESCHOOLING BESTSELLER!

"If you can afford only one resource directory,
this is the one to buy."—Library Journal

Available at bookstores and libraries.